LIVE SMART RETIRE RICH

To Margaret, All the best Dan [illegible]

Learn The Secrets That The Wealthy Use To Secure Your Own Financial Future Now!

LIVE SMART RETIRE RICH

Learn the Secrets that the Wealthy Use to Secure Your Own Financial Future Now!

Daniel C. Goodwin

BRAND ARTIST PRESS

Published by: Brand Artist Press, Inc. 525 Athens Place, Westfield, IN 46074
Design by: The Brand Artist, Inc. (www.thebrandartist.com)

Printed in the United States of America

ISBN 10: 0-61533-953-0
ISBN 13: 978-0-615-33953-5

For my wife, Kim, my daughter,
Rachel, and my son, Ben,
and for every American who wants and
needs a personal financial plan.

CONTENTS

About the Author

Daniel C. Goodwin has a passion for teaching others how to increase their fiscal literacy. Daniel began a career in real estate in 1984 that led to the ownership of a finance organization that has funded over half a billion dollars in business. Starting with nothing, Daniel has created a seven-figure personal portfolio that includes the basics—such as commercial, residential, and development real estate; IRAs and 401(k)s; mutual funds; life insurance; annuities; and stocks—as well as the most complex and sophisticated derivative money strategies and hedging techniques available on Wall Street. Daniel subscribes to a team concept of personal finance, similar to what you might find in the boardroom, operating room, football huddle, orchestra, or construction site. In 2004, Daniel founded the Texas Continued Education Institute. The organization's mission is to bring relevant financial education concepts and strategies to those who have a need and desire to learn. TCEI workshops and educational materials, including this book, enlist the time and expertise of tax attorneys, asset managers, certified mortgage planners, trust officers, private bankers, estate planning attorneys, and a host of other financial professionals working together to make a difference in communities across America. Daniel is also a published author and a regular speaker in his hometown of The Woodlands, Texas.

Daniel's gift is taking the complex and making it simple. For more information and a speaking schedule go to www.WeRetireWell.com.

Additional copies of this book are available online at Amazon.com, BarnesandNoble.com, and Borders.com.

Introduction

I have written this book because I am alarmed for many Americans. While I have employed planning, strategies, discipline, and structure to safeguard the personal finances of many families, including my own, I am keenly aware that in America most people have not taken similar steps. According to statistics, only two in five people are on track for a financially sound retirement. Far too many people in this great land of ours, as many as 180 million Americans, are not ready for the future ahead of them. Too many of our country's heroes—our servicemen and women, teachers, and law enforcement officers—will face dire financial circumstances in their golden years as living costs rise, investments falter, and incomes diminish. Too many parents are not empowered to teach their children financial principles; they cannot give their children what they do not possess themselves. Too many people quietly avoid going to that back corner of their minds where frightening questions like these may be lurking:

1. Am I on the right financial path and investing properly?

2. Will I outlive my money or become a burden to my children?

3. Have I kept up with the changes to our tax code? Do I understand their implications and effects on the quality of my retirement?

4. Am I meeting my stewardship responsibilities to personal finance and community?

5. Have I learned not just to work for my money but have my money work for me?

6. Do I really understand the importance of cash flow, leverage, arbitrage, compounding, and other important money management concepts?

7. Am I in a position to teach my children fiscal literacy?

8. Have I kept up my financial education over the years or have I outsourced this responsibility to others with dismal results?

9. Have I questioned my current advisors' motives?

10. Do I have a personal money plan that provides peace of mind, clarity, synergy, and accountability?

Most of us are experts in our chosen vocations. One of my clients, Ann, graduated at the top of her class at a prestigious law school and has a vibrant law practice. Her husband writes university-level textbooks. In my book, that makes them both pretty smart. Their accomplishments took years of training, experience, and sacrifice. Ann would tell you, however, that money and investing have just never interested her that much. She is far more interested in her law career and quality time with her husband, children, and grandchildren. Ann and her husband have a team of experts designing their strategies for wealth creation and preservation because they understand that being brilliant in your career as an attorney, surgeon, educator, engineer, or homemaker does not mean you are good with money. I know many doctors who are practicing medicine far too late in life because they lacked fiscal literacy earlier in their careers and now have to work to put food on the table in their sixties and even seventies. Despite having the brains to make it through the rigor of medical school, many found that dealing with money involves a whole different learning curve.

The truth is most of us are just busy with life—our careers, travel, hobbies, church activities, family obligations, volunteer work, and more. We have lunches to make and meetings to prepare for. We have bills to pay and teachers to conference with. We have cars that are long overdue for oil changes and need to be washed. We want to be good parents, to read with our children and mentor them. We have scrapbooks to finish, television shows to catch up on, and current events to keep up with. Because we go, go, go, we need to find time for some quality relaxation and entertainment like enjoying a good football game or watching Tiger take apart a field of lesser opponents. But we *still* need to get to the gym, cut the grass, and respond to twenty e-mails. Man, are we busy!

So, what do we do about money? Chances are that we have a neighbor who is a "financial advisor." We decide to give him a try, or we grab a copy of *Smart Money* on our next flight to Cleveland and read all of the latest and greatest advice on building wealth. We may say, "Hey, I can do that!" and become a do-it-yourselfer with all of our extra time; or we may just take a leap of faith with an advisor we feel pretty good about even though we secretly wonder if our investments reflect the firm's agenda more than our own. We read our investment statements and scratch our heads, but we know deep down that we are not on course for financial independence.

If you are currently knocking the ball out of the park financially, this book may not be for you. (Note: "knocking the ball out of the park" is not to be confused with earning large sums of money.) We have all seen the celebrities of the world who earn hundreds of millions of dollars during their careers only to blow up later in life and file bankruptcy. Go figure. NFL teams have been sold under duress because "big earners" with big egos proved to be poor money managers and planners. Any amount of money—no matter how large—can be blown and squandered.

If you have clear answers to all the questions listed at the beginning of this chapter, I do not want to waste your time with this book. You are likely in the top 3 percent of Americans with respect to fiscal literacy. I wrote this book for the other 97 percent. I have read the personal financial statements, tax returns, credit reports, and investment statements of thousands of families over the past twenty years. I know what kind of shape we are in as a nation with personal finance. I know many of our families have negative savings rates and are not on track for the financial demands the future will hold. I know that most of the traditional "over-the-counter" financial planning methods have failed millions of Americans.

During years of running my own financial services firm, I watched thousands of families "bare all" to get approved to finance real estate. Because so many families I have come into contact with need help in personal finance, I founded the Texas Continued Education Institute in 2004. The mission of this organization is to bring relevant financial and educational concepts and strategies to those who have a need and desire to learn. TCEI workshops enlist the time and expertise of Board Certified tax attorneys, asset managers, certified mortgage planners, trust officers, private bankers, estate planning attorneys, and a host of other professionals who want to make a difference in our community. I am proud to say that this book leverages the knowledge, education, expertise, and strategies of many.

Are you one of the millions of Americans who needs some help with money? Are you ready to open your mind and suspend your fears regarding personal finance? Do you want and need a plan? If your answer is yes, if you feel like you and your family deserve the future you've been dreaming of, then I am honored and privileged to say that I have written this book for you!

Daniel C. Goodwin

Entrepreneur, Educator, Real Estate Developer, and Investor and Founder of the Texas Continued Education Institute

Chapter One

Know the Why

All the perplexities, confusion and distress in America arise not from defects in their Constitution or Confederation, nor from want of honor or virtue, so much as downright ignorance of the nature of coin, credit, and circulation.

~John Adams

Before we dive into the reasons for this book, I want to ask you *why*. Why are you reading this book? What are your primary concerns and interests relating to money and the concepts we will cover together? What do you hope to gain as a result of investing your time with the subject matter? I know that in life all of our personal radio stations are tuned in to WIIFM: "What's in it for me?"

So, what is in it for you? Ponder this for just a moment. Are you behind on getting your financial act together? Are you a super-achiever who is smart enough to know that there is always more to learn? Are you feeling let down by the establishment's view on personal finance, and do you think the job is just not getting done? Do you think you should be further along with money at this point in your life? Are you an up-and-coming, energetic young person who wants to avoid the financial mistakes that millions of Americans are currently making? Is your anxiety rising as you creep closer to retirement while the weight of finances looms larger every day?

Take a moment to reflect upon at least three of the money-related concerns (or opportunities, depending on how you look at things) listed below. Do not put this off, as this exercise will be important for you to get the most from this book and the strategies it contains. It is important to reflect on what is important to you right now. Ask yourself how you are doing right now in these areas:

- Asset allocation
- Asset protection
- Charitable giving
- College planning
- Estate planning

- Financial planning
- Getting out of debt
- Income / distribution
- Investing in real estate
- Life insurance
- Outliving your money
- Retirement planning
- Stocks, options, and hedging
- Tax avoidance strategies
- Wealth creation

Whatever your circumstances and concerns (or opportunities) are, you are reading this book now; and for that I am grateful, and I commend you. You are part of the minority. The vast majority of Americans is asleep at the wheel and will perpetuate the statistics we all see regularly regarding money and readiness. My promise to you is to be a good steward of our time together. This book will help you get on a better path. By applying the simple, time-tested, and proven concepts taught in the following chapters you will find clarity, peace, and the resolution of many of your financial concerns.

Nothing in my life has impacted me more than the tears I have seen fall from clients' eyes when heavy burdens of worry and fear related to personal finance have been lifted from their shoulders. Some have never before had sound financial plans structured by advisors collaborating to achieve the goals envisioned by their families—plans that could forever change their futures and outlooks on life. Others find renewed confidence in knowing they no longer need to fear outliving their money. Some find peace in knowing that their plans were built around their family agendas, definitions of financial success, and legacies, and not the agendas of banks, insurance companies, wire houses, financial advisors, or loan officers. I also find great satisfaction when I work with young, ambitious, motivated people who early in life chose to reject mediocrity and have already learned that education, innovation, collaboration, and creativity are the currency of the future.

What I am advocating here is a team approach to planning, which enlists the expertise of several advisors, each of whom is an expert in his or her chosen field. The team has a quarterback, of course—that's you. At a minimum, the team should have a tax attorney, asset manager, CPA, insurance professional, estate planning attorney, and debt strategist. These parties represent the advisory pillars for those with a high net worth, the most affluent Americans. A team approach is the expected norm in this world, unlike in Middle America. Did you know that you and I can have such a team without shelling out megabucks? Did you know we all deserve a dream team? Do you have such a team now, or are you following a trail blazed by the masses? This book will show you how to assemble a team of your own and put it to work for you with relative ease. You just have to know what questions to ask of whom and what instructions the quarterback will give. Think of yourself as the team owner. Everyone on the team works for you!

With the many uncertainties in today's new global economy, we have reason to harbor financial doubt and fear in some regard, either for ourselves or our loved ones regarding money, debt, retirement, and personal finances. Here are some noteworthy statistics:

- Consumer debt has doubled in the past twenty years with the average family credit card debt standing at over nine thousand dollars as of 2009. The average interest rate on this credit card debt stands at 18.9 percent. Making only the minimum payments on this debt, these families will need thirty-six years to pay off their credit cards.

- Thirty-four percent of workers surveyed responded that they would have to guess to estimate how much money they would need to save for retirement.
- Personal savings rates have fallen to a negative number for the fist time in our nation's history, down from 10 percent in the 1980s.
- Outstanding household debt stands at over ten trillion dollars, doubling since 1992.
- Forty percent of Americans spend more annually than their net earnings.
- Median household income has risen only 11 percent since 1990, while the cost of living over the same period has risen almost 30 percent.
- Thirty percent of workers say they have not saved a dime for retirement.
- Two-thirds of households have less than ten thousand dollars saved.
- Sixty-three percent of Americans do not have a financial advisor or financial plan of any kind. Thirty-seven percent of

Americans have mortgages that are not suited to their risk tolerance.

- Ninety-seven percent of Americans do not have a team of advisors working on their behalf in a collaborative effort to structure and orchestrate their financial and tax planning strategies.

Mass marketing has effectively convinced most of us that we need plasma TVs, the latest iPods, sports cars, homes in neighborhoods we really can't afford, and tropical vacations. We have the best clothes, makeup, computers, and designer sunglasses. Going out to eat is now a standard part of the American lifestyle, as are travel sports for our kids, yearly birthday parties, and nine or ten dollar movie tickets. We now have cell phone plans and high-speed Internet bills to add to our monthly expenses. We are spending like there is no tomorrow, but deep inside, we know there is.

The American consumer engine is the largest in the free world. America consumes approximately 25 percent of the world's goods, services, and products, despite representing only 5 percent of the world's population. Consumerism is alive and well in America; all the while, fiscal literacy, investment, and retirement planning languish for many.

What is wrong with many of us? Do we feel it is our birthright to experience a serene and well-financed retirement, even without doing anything to ensure that it will happen? Is there some retirement fairy that I have never heard of?

In my own family, as I was growing up, there was always a shortage of money. Perhaps that is what motivated me to make sure that, unlike my father, if I was working at age seventy, it would be because I wanted to and not because I had to. I fear for so many young people today, as well as for my own children, who have never experienced anything but prosperity. Will they have the drive to go out and make it on their own? Have they been crippled by affluence, abundance, and everything coming so easily? Because we love our children so much, my wife and I have set out to make sure that this does not happen in our home. In the chapter to come on kids and money, I will spell out some real-life truths and strategies to help you make sure your kids are not ill-equipped when it comes to taking on life, money, and the knowledge they will need to succeed.

My kids operate bank accounts and investment funds and have learned basic cash flow management skills. They work and earn their own spending money. They understand what assets and liabilities are, as well as the value of saving and tracking their money. My wife and I explain taxes to our kids and what our family bills amount to. We impose penalties for poor financial decisions. We love our children far too much to leave these things to chance and hope that they will figure them all on their own somehow.

Wake Up and Smell the Coffee

We need to wake up. The money and retirement game has completely changed. Our parents and grandparents could rely on the three-legged-stool method for retirement planning. It looked like this:

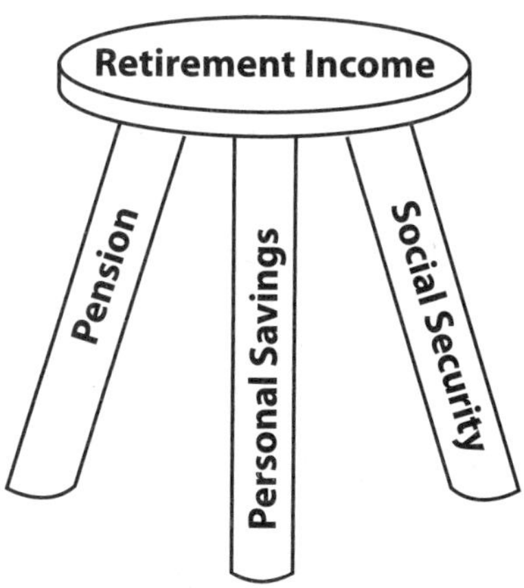

Today's retirement planning looks more like this:

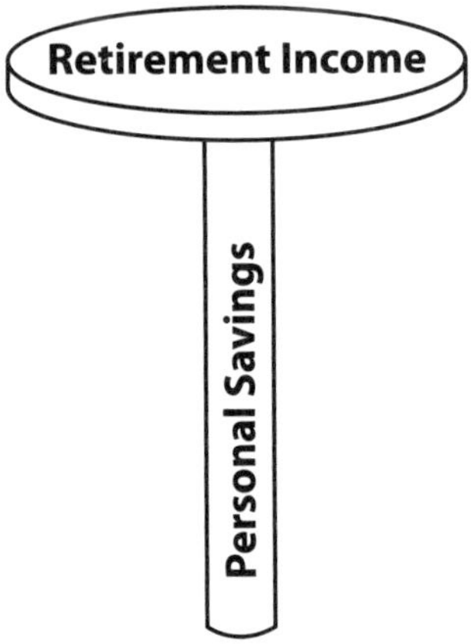

It's now *your* savings you're depending on, not that of the government or your employer.

Unlike you and me, our parents and grandparents went to work for companies with pension plans; they usually retired thirty years later and could depend on two legs (pension and Social Security) that are either gone today or may be gone in the future. In the 1960s and 1970s, pension plans began to cost too much for companies to remain competitive in a global economy, and sadly, today, they are primarily a thing of the past.

Many younger workers don't even know what a pension is. Well, here's a newsflash for you: Foreign automakers and other foreign firms do not fund their workers' retirements. They never have. Workers in other countries save and plan for their own retirements. Do you think this helps foreign companies to be more competitive? Does this give you any idea why Toyota and Honda are crushing our great legacy companies like GM and Ford? Pension plans are a relic of the past for most people, and those who still have pensions may face the restructuring of faltering plans. In short, there is not much confidence to be found today in most existing pension plans.

What about Social Security?

In my lectures, I ask attendees to raise their hands if they have confidence that they will receive their Social Security benefits upon retirement. Sadly, it is rare that a hand goes up. And why expect any different? We all know that Social Security is approaching bankruptcy. This dirty little secret is not so secret any more. By 2015, Social Security will be paying more in benefits than it collects in taxes, and by 2039, given current benefits formulas and tax rates, the Social Security Trust Fund will be exhausted (Board of Trustees 2000, p. 27).

We know that we have been lied to and that the boxes of IOUs cannot possibly withstand the pressure of eighty million baby boomers moving from the paying end of the line to the receiving end. To top it all off, we are living longer. If you make it to age sixty-five today you have a one in four chance of living to one hundred. We know that if we have saved anything for retirement, Social Security will likely tell us that there are others who need Social Security benefits more than we do, and they will be telling the truth. The government cannot give you what they do not have regardless of whether Social Security benefits were previously promised to you. I believe it to be naïve, wishful thinking—some call it "head-in-the-sand thinking"—to hope that Congress will somehow save us.

401(k)s

In 1974, Congress passed ERISA, the Employee Retirement Income Security Act. This is where we got our 401(k)s and IRA's. I will discuss in greater detail in another chapter the pros and cons of 401(k)s and some 401(k) planning strategies. Suffice it to say at this time that this is your gift from Congress to get after your own retirement planning—and get after it, you must. Right about the time ERISA took effect, Americans first heard of the mutual fund. I will have much to say about mutual funds later in the book and how millions are trapped in some of the worst, tax-inefficient, and most commonly pedaled vehicles on the planet. They are the default path of the masses, as there are currently more mutual funds on Wall Street than there are stocks! Do you think this mass force has a voice? Do you think this voice has an agenda? Are you comfortable that this agenda is the same as your family's agenda? I'm not!

Pressure

Today, we experience significant pressures that our parents and grandparents did not face, including becoming less valuable to our companies as we age, caring for aging parents, living longer, and supporting children who have returned to the nest, unable to make it on their own. Some families have to deal with many of these pressures at the same time. Additional pressures include corporate downsizing and companies filling positions with younger workers who can be promised the sun, the moon, and the stars, and who will gladly accept wages that cannot sustain their older counterparts' families and lifestyles.

We face major pressures with our money and the complexity of learning to invest for our futures. This is most bothersome to me when most of the financial advice that I see churned and recycled from Wall Street—much of it confusing and contradictory—comes from the investment firms who have their own agendas in mind for our futures. We are the first generation of Americans who will have to say, "The buck stops with us," when it comes to retirement. Are we ready? Most Americans have never received any education on money strategies, formal, informal, or otherwise. Our employers' 401(k)s and self-contained mutual funds are not a good enough plan for retirement. The math is fairly easy on this.

Hang in There

We have been told to "just hang in there" with our mutual funds and 401(k)s as we watch them languish. But if we have any experience at all in the mutual fund gambit, we know it's a glorified crapshoot. We can all recall the losses just a short time ago in our 401(k)s. Most of this advice to be patient comes from financial advisors who may or may not have two dimes to rub together themselves but act as if they have the wisdom of the ages for you and me. I strongly caution the readers of this book against taking advice from advisors whom you know do not have the net worth that you have. What's wrong with asking an advisor what his income, net worth, and personal investments amount to? This may seem bold, intrusive, or forward, but I do not mind it one bit when I'm asked for these details. The advisor is asking you for all of your information, right? Do not take advice from novices who are incompetent or lack life experience and stature in their field. I seek out advisors with clients who are far wealthier than I am and who have reached the highest levels of success among their peers. To do the same, you have to ask questions and be bold. This book will show you how.

The Rich Get Richer

This can be disturbing, especially when we know that the wealthy employ tools, investments, and money strategies that Middle America never has the chance to participate in. I have news for you: people with five to ten million dollars deposited with blue chip Wall Street firms have another world of investment choices and options at their disposal. They are taken into the finest boardrooms where the firms' top teams of senior advisors, each with their own areas of expertise, are introduced. Everyone says, "Yes, sir," and "Can I get you something, Ms. So-and-so?" These advisors are the elite, the most astute, accomplished, and sophisticated. They handle money for the wealthy. They could name-drop about who their clients are, but they would never compromise their clients' confidentiality. They produce results that are far superior to—often many times greater than—those attained through the advice, strategy, and structure that Middle America has access to, minus the risk. They effectively eliminate losses to their investors without removing the upside potential by utilizing complex and sophisticated hedging and derivative monetization strategies. They entirely change the risk-reward paradigm, while optimizing investment performance, tax minimization, asset protection, and estate planning.

Most wealthy people never lose money when the markets go down. They don't have to. We all know they employ legal methods to virtually eliminate most taxes. They approach real estate, borrowing, and taxes from a counterintuitive perspective unknown to most Americans. They do things differently than Middle America. Let me say that in another way: The wealthy are playing a different game with a different set of rules. Most Americans are playing checkers while the wealthy are playing chess.

Most Americans are told to simply diversify and hang in there; they are pointed to the chart on the wall of the eighty-year S&P or some other symbol that suggests that they will be fine in the future. The common desire seems to be to sell the investment that requires the least effort to explain or that pays the most to the advisor. I say don't bet your future on investments like those. What if you could invest and plan like the wealthy? What if we could all remove the down years? What if we could learn to minimize taxes—legally? If you could take advantage of the same tax shelters the wealthiest Americans use, and pay less in taxes, wouldn't you want to? This book will show you how.

Case in Point

Many people are familiar with Dallas Mavericks owner Mark Cuban who sold his company to Yahoo! for billions and was paid out in Yahoo! stock. The stock was trading at about 250 dollars per share and later fell to less than 10 dollars per share during the dot-com bust, yet Mark Cuban retained his billions. You and I would have been (and may indeed have been) road kill if our 401(k) mutual funds owned Yahoo! stock, but Wall Street designed a hedging strategy to preserve their richest clients' wealth. Did you know that you and I can employ such strategies? Did you know that we do not have to factor in losing our money with market volatility if we do not want to? You have many other choices to building wealth and paying less in taxes than you are currently utilizing. After reading this book you will be informed so that you can make such choices. I believe you will be motivated and educated to follow Warren Buffett's rules of investing:

> *"Rule #1 – Never lose your money. Rule #2 – Never forget Rule #1."*

One more important note: you cannot afford losses. If your investment loses 50 percent of its value then has a 50 percent gain, you'll be back to even with your money, right? WRONG. You will still be 25 percent in the hole after 2 years, not counting your opportunity cost.

Here's an example:

$100,000 50% loss = $50,000 Then, $50,000 + 50% gain ($25,000) = $75,000

After two years, a 50 percent loss and a subsequent 50 percent gain, you are now in the red by 25 percent from where you started. With a down 50% year followed by an up 50% year most people would think you would be even, but you're not. Your still down 25% !!

This is the buy-diversify-and-wait strategy of investing in mutual funds. The trouble is that you are probably still waiting and waiting and waiting. Many Americans don't even bother opening their investment statements anymore.

Get Real

I am going to get real in this book. I am not going to show you how to get wealthy by skipping your morning Starbucks trip. I would rather have the Starbucks! I am not going to help you get rich in real estate by profiting from others' hardships and misfortune. I would rather see you in a position to lend a helping hand to someone in need. I am not going to advise you to quit your job, start a franchise, or get involved in multi-level marketing. I would rather see you optimize the resources and strategies that are currently available to you and every other American right now. I would rather see you learn how to earn more in passive income. I am not going to recycle the same old worn-out advice posted on all of the Internet financial pages. Instead this book will teach you real multimillionaire monetization strategies that harness the power of leverage, arbitrage, compounding, asset protection, real estate, finance, and tax minimization. This book will teach you how ordinary Americans like you and me can employ the financial tools and strategies that are common to the wealthy.

Multimillionaires do things differently than most. The biggest difference between the wealthy and the masses is that the wealthy refuse to accept the norm as the default path with their investments and strategies. They are optimistic and believe there are always better ideas. They harness the knowledge of others and have a voracious appetite for learning and personal growth. The money is not the main goal; excellence is. The money just seems to follow.

In the chapters to come, I will show you how to change the rules of the game and how to employ the strategies of the wealthy regardless of your current net worth. Financial rules can be bent to your will and favor—legally, morally, and ethically—if you have the formula. Multimillionaires have been doing it for years. Now it's your time!

I am going to ask you to go out on a limb a bit and reflect upon three things that you would do in your lifetime if money and finances were not an issue. Go ahead and dream—dream big. Do it for you. Do it for your family. It might be taking a trip around the world, building a home, or funding an organization. It could be starting a business, pursuing a degree, buying a new wardrobe or car, purchasing a company, or supporting a place of worship. Go ahead and do it now.

Spend at least ten minutes reflecting on three or more dreams that complete financial security would allow you to pursue.

> *Twenty years from now you will be more disappointed by the things that you didn't do than by the ones you did do. So throw off the bowlines. Sail away from the safe harbor. Catch the trade winds in your sails. Explore. Dream. Discover.*
>
> ~Mark Twain

> *All men dream but not equally. Those who dream by night in the dusty recesses of their minds wake in the day to find that it was vanity; but the dreamers of the day are dangerous men, for they may act their dream with open eyes to make it possible.*
>
> ~T. E. Lawrence

Chapter Two

Managing Family Cash Flow Like a Business

Chains of habit are too light to be felt until they are too heavy to be broken.

~ Warren Buffett

While any credible business has financial statements, few families do. A company needs to be able to quickly view its P&L (profit and loss) and balance sheet (assets and liabilities). These statements quickly tell the reader about the health of the company, the company's financial strength or weakness, and what the company's value might be. These reports can also help in determining how much money a company can borrow from a bank. Over time, a company's ability to successfully manage income and expenses, as well as assets and liabilities, determines the financial success and strength of the company. The same principals are true for your family and for my family.

Profit & Loss Statements

The P&L (profit and loss) statement is a statement of how much money is coming into the business each month and how much is leaving the business each month. If the company is earning a profit, or has a surplus, the figure at the bottom of the report is in black ink. (The company is profitable or "in the black.") If the company is losing money, the figure at the bottom is in red ink, indicating a loss. The P&L is the accepted accounting tool businesses use to know their numbers and to plan and adjust strategy accordingly. Few families really know or have any method for seeing what their true income and expenses amount to. It has been estimated that less than one in ten households operates under any sort of budget or method of assessing how the family is managing income and expenses.

Cash Flow Management

Managing cash flow means controlling the amount of money that comes into and leaves your bank account each month. The simple goal in managing cash flow is to create a surplus. That surplus is then allocated into investments that will make you financially secure over time. I believe that for families managing cash flow is as important as it is for a Fortune 500 company. After all, are you more concerned with your family's financial health or Exxon Mobil's?

Most people I know think of cash flow management as budgeting and would rather eat a cockroach than go on a budget. In simple terms, a budget sets aside certain amounts of money each month for different expense categories, including all necessary and discretionary expenses. "Budgets don't feel good." "Budgets are restrictive." "Budgets make you feel like a pauper." "Budgets cramp our style." "Budgets don't let you live in the moment." "Budgets feel like grown-up allowance" That's how people think, right? The reality is that while most people do not say any of those things out loud, they quietly avoid budgeting and ignore the fact that each month they slip further and further from their dreams and any degree of financial solvency. This generally is where the credit cards and home equity loans come into play, further compounding—and not addressing—the real problem of cash flow management and family P&L. "You only live once." "You can't take it with you." "Money can't buy happiness" "I don't want to be controlled by money." These are all common laments and excuses for people who do not want to face the reality of managing their income and expenses. This story is far too common with big earners as well as those who really work hard just to make ends meet. When companies ignore their P&Ls over time they eventually go bankrupt and are consumed by their competitors. When you and I ignore our family P&Ls, over time we grow into dysfunctional money traps, robbed of our future and exposed to dangerous and painful risks.

I worked with a client recently who made close to three hundred thousand dollars in income per year but whose family spent as much money each month as was coming in to support a large mortgage, a second home, private schools, dirt bikes, boats, jewelry, vacations, hundred-dollar dinners, large SUVs, and an appetite for the finest clothes. Their spoiled kids thought they were rich, too, as they owned all of the latest and coolest electronics, cell phones, dirt bikes and toys.

You've got the picture, right? The family had two boys headed to college in two years with no money put away to pay for it, no real retirement savings or planning, no life or disability insurance, and no real emergency fund—but, man, did they look good to the Joneses. In fact for all appearances this family was kicking the Joneses' you-know-what. For some odd reason I almost thought I could hear a time bomb ticking as I grasped the reality of the situation.

All of their friends thought the family was wealthy because of the gorgeous home and all the toys, but a financial statement quickly revealed that the family was broke. The irony was that my client saw himself as wealthy. The family's liabilities were almost as much as their assets, but the client just saw all of the luxury toys and assumed he was wealthy. As you might guess, just like in the emergency room, the first task at hand was to stop the bleeding, and that can be painful. It is much easier to stick our heads in the sand and hope that somehow our problems go away and that one day our ship will come in. Unfortunately, that ship is likely to be a broken-down rowboat with holes in the bottom, not the luxury cruise liner that we had envisioned for our retirement. Facing your realities, your family P&L, can be painful but also liberating. It takes much courage. The reality is that some will but most won't. You can! I say forget the Joneses. I heard someone once say that in America too often we spend money that we don't have to buy things that we don't need to impress people that we don't like. Go figure.

Budgeting

Budgeting has never appealed to me, and I do not recommend it for myself, or for you. *Say what?* Let me say that another way. I believe that every budget out there is designed for failure, and I have seen lots of systems: envelopes, family contracts and blood oaths, convoluted software systems, and more. I have seen many budgets do more harm than good. They don't work. How can this be, you ask? What kind of quack are you anyway? You call yourself a financial expert and you are not on a budget?

Correct. I am not on a budget, nor do I recommend one for you. I do however manage cash flow, and I recommend that you do the same. By managing cash flow, you can be successful at what budgets attempt to do but fail miserably at. Remember what I said about that cockroach. People fail at budgets almost 100 percent of the time. Successful cash flow management is the natural result of knowing your numbers. Successful cash flow management can bring a family together, while a budget can tear a family apart. As you might already know, money causes more strife in families than any other single issue and is the cause of more divorces than I care to throw a statistic at.

In sports one of the key differences between a professional and an amateur is that a professional knows his numbers. When a major league batter comes to bat, his career performance and production are flashed on the Jumbotron for all to see. His numbers represent how well he has achieved his goal of hitting pitches. The same is true for you and for me with our family finances and investments. Our families' P&Ls give us vivid pictures of our cash flow management results. Right now you and I are either winning or losing at this important endeavor. Think of the P&L as a report card for grownups. You likely push your kids to do their best in school and make As or the very best grades that they can, right? Why not take some of your own advice and put the family finances and future on a firm foundation. Can you say right now that you are doing your very best? Would you get an A if your CPA came into your home and graded you on cash flow management, or would your kids see you getting Cs or Ds? Are you preaching one thing about effort and success yet doing another? You must master this principle before learning about real estate, investments, tax strategies, and estate planning in the chapters to come.

Learning Our Numbers

We learn what our numbers are first, and then modify our behavior as the natural result of our newfound awareness. You might be surprised to find out how simple and liberating this is. Instead of swearing a blood oath that I will only go to the movies once a month and rather than checking an envelope only to find no money there, I spend about an hour a month reviewing my income and expenses from the previous month. If I was over budget that month I make certain modifications to my family P&L. This could be to make more money the following month or to spend less, or both. My review could also show that the family has a surplus, which would lead to a decision as to where that surplus should be invested. What a great way for a husband and wife to come together, reviewing the family's progress toward reaching their goals. This can be a good feeling, one you will want to repeat. Being in the red (showing a loss for the month) is a bad feeling, and one you will instinctively avoid if you know and regularly review your numbers. No one wants to blow it two months in a row. Learning what your income and expenses are can take up all of about one hour per month. Your actions and spending habits will be shaped by your knowledge and awareness of your family P&L instead of a budget that is destined to fail. The bottom line is this: cash flow management works, and budgets do not.

Pay Yourself First

One reason the government does not trust us to just pay our taxes all in one lump sum at the end of the year is that it knows it would not get the money. Collecting taxes with every check ensures that the government will in fact get paid. Here is one place I give our government an A+, and I want you to apply this same simple concept to your family cash flow management P&L. When you "pay yourself first" you ensure that your family P&L will reserve a portion of your income each month for the most important financial allocations, such as accumulating funds to build your reserve account, giving, and investing wisely. I want you to set up a draft from your checking account that pulls a percentage of your net income every month from your checking account and puts it into a money market fund. These drafts are cumbersome to undo once you set them up, so my bet is that you will make sure the money is in your checking account each month to cover the draft. This simple process will become a discipline that will automatically propel you closer each month to your financial freedom date, when you will finally be doing what you want with your time! Some of you may have read *The Richest Man in Babylon* by George S. Clason, which has maintained shelf space at major bookstores since 1928. This book tells the story of one man building a lifetime of riches with simple, time-tested formulas like paying yourself first. I would recommend *The Richest Man in Babylon* to anyone who wants to ensure that they master cash flow management as a family lifestyle. For a cash flow management form (P&L) that you and your family can use each month to better understand your income and expenses go to www.WeRetireWell.com. You can also find many other good cash flow management tools and calculators on the Internet. There is a sample included at the end of this chapter.

Creating a Reserve Account

After you have decided on and implemented a strategy to produce and review a monthly family P&L and to manage cash flow, the next task on your must-do list will be establishing a reserve account. The advice and planning on this topic may seem boring and old-fashioned to some, but it is critically important. A reserve account is a fund that should be equal to three to six months of living and expenses. As we all know, emergencies happen. When they do, will you have a fund to access, or will you do what most Americans do and reach for the plastic? Maintaining a reserve account can dovetail nicely into your cash flow management strategy. When you review your family P&L each month, you can allocate funds to first build the reserve account and then to replenish it as needed when you have had to access it for emergencies or overruns that may have pushed your P&L into the red for a month. You should have your reserve account balance on hand as you monitor your family P&L each month. I keep a reserve account on deposit at a local bank, and I recommend that you do the same. While I prefer a bank that I can walk into, I have no issue with you finding the best rates on the Net and setting up an account with any of the reputable online institutions. Use your reserve account for things like ER visits with the kids, once-in-a-lifetime vacations, car repairs, speeding tickets, a new computer to replace one that has crashed and burned, home repairs, and the sorts of nonrecurring expenses that can blow a hole in your monthly cash flow statements.

A Lifetime of Habits

I truly believe that in our later years, when we measure our effectiveness with finances and money, our success will depend more on a lifetime of habits rather than on whether we earned 8 percent in this account or 12 percent in another. People who effectively manage cash flow over their lifetimes have a quality of retirement that is virtually assured, even if they made some subpar investment choices. It really is a matter of mastering your habits.

Managing cash flow is a habit. Maintaining an emergency fund and not relying on plastic is a habit. Avoiding dumb debt, setting goals, and increasing fiscal literacy on a regular basis are all habits. These habits will become the foundation and character of all that you do in personal finance and investing and, over a lifetime, will make you rich.

> *Sow a thought and you reap an act; sow an act and you reap a habit; sow a habit and you reap a character; sow a character and you reap a destiny.*
>
> ~Charles Reader

No Dumb Debt

"No dumb debt" is a mantra that can pay off in spades over a lifetime. It means that the only debt that you should ever carry is a mortgage, a business loan (if you are self-employed), or perhaps one car loan at a time. Your P&L will quickly show you that you will have more money to invest if you are conservative with car expenses. I drove a Chevy truck for about 160,000 miles and loved every minute of it. The money that could have gone into fancy cars was being diverted into tax-free investment accounts and real estate. I saw guys going by in BMWs with nine-hundred-dollar lease payments and just grinned.

Credit card debt should make you want to throw up. It says, "I never saw value in creating an emergency fund, and I prefer for my family's money to go to Visa rather than into investments for our future." It also indicates that you do not mind paying ridiculous amounts of interest on consumer goods and that your fiscal literacy is low. If you have dumb debt now, get rid of it; and if necessary, get rid of the card, too. I carry credit cards because I do not carry dumb debt. If you have a problem with dumb debt, then perhaps you should not carry credit cards. Instead, just use a debit card and make sure in advance that you can use it to rent a car if needed. Do not finance furniture, televisions, computers, vacations, or any other consumer item with plastic or E-Z credit terms. Pay for these items from your reserve account.

If you need more help in getting out of debt than this chapter offers, consider reading *How to Get Out of Debt, Stay Out of Debt, and Live Prosperously* by Jerrold Mundis. You *must* avoid all of the debt consolidation services, lenders, and companies who would make you believe that your debt is not your fault and that they can simply wave some magic wand and cure all of your problems with some product or service they are selling. These firms will ruin your credit, rob the equity from your home, and ignore your real problems, the ones that got you into the mess to begin with. Trust me on this. These types of "debt counselors," as they like to call themselves, are wolves in sheep's clothing, and that includes home equity lenders, Consumer Credit Counseling Service (CCCS), and all of the other supposed Good Samaritans who "just want to help." Think about it. People fail to manage cash flow, and then they charge up credit cards that get paid off with home equity loans. You can only do this for a little while, before as they sat back home "the chickens come home to roost". After the home equity well runs dry, there will be plenty of bankruptcy attorneys who have your best interest in mind, too, if you believe that. This story is far too common in America. It truly saddens me and is clear evidence of our nation's lack of fiscal literacy.

Goals

While this is not a book on goal-setting, it is hard to think about financial success, security, and independence without having clearly defined goals. I believe if you start with fuzzy and vague goals then you will get fuzzy, vague, and ineffective results with your money.

> *Our plans miscarry because they have no aim. When a man does not know what harbor he is making for, no wind is the right wind.*
>
> ~Seneca

To be successful with your money you must first have a desire and then a vision. Goals, strategies, discipline, and structure will follow. Think of Steven Covey's second habit: begin with the end in mind. Covey states that when we begin with the end in mind we have a personal direction to guide our daily activities, without which we would accomplish little toward our own goals. Beginning with the end in mind is part of the process of personal leadership, taking control of our own lives. So, set your goals. Write them down, and be specific. I challenge you to do it. If you want the wisdom of an expert on goal-setting, read any of the books on goals by Zig Ziglar or Brian Tracy.

In closing this chapter I want to tell you about another family that I was fortunate enough to meet at my practice in The Woodlands, Texas; I'll call them Sam and Lisa. Sam and Lisa asked our firm for advice about financing a new home. I noticed that the home was a conservative purchase relative to their income per underwriting guidelines. They explained that they had their own family guidelines, and it was evident that they knew what they could and could not afford. Sam and Lisa had no interest in buying a larger or more expensive home just because some lender said that they could be approved for a larger loan.

Sam and Lisa had been coached about money. In reviewing Sam and Lisa's personal financial statement I quickly noticed that the only debt that they carried was a mortgage. Sam explained that they paid cash for all other expenses and that they had a family method for controlling expenses and allocating income. The mortgage Sam and Lisa selected was interest only, and Lisa explained that this was because they wanted to put the least amount down so they could avoid mortgage insurance and waive escrows. Sam and Lisa explained that they had been successful in not paying down mortgages and using their cash surpluses to invest in other real estate and certain principal-protected structured investments through their financial planner. Sam and Lisa had a reserve fund with about forty thousand dollars, and their real estate and other investments were growing at a very nice rate. Lisa explained that, for them, managing money was like tending to a garden; they worked in their garden so that it would bear fruit. I was impressed with her words. Sam and Lisa had average jobs and income. It was what they were doing outside of their jobs that were making them rich.

Sam and Lisa had four other real estate investments and were moving into the commercial real estate arena as they had become bored with controlling rental properties.

Sam and Lisa had hired a bookkeeper who was under the direction of a CPA who was under the direction of a tax attorney. I could see from their real estate portfolio that they had learned about leverage, arbitrage, compounding, and the many tax-favored strategies that could make them wealthy. Sam told me that their other non-real-estate assets were doing very well because they had figured out how to move into structured assets that would not go down when the market went down. Sam was smart enough to learn that losses kill long-term performance, and he had a clear understanding about compounding money. Sam and Lisa only contributed to their 401(k) an amount equal to their employers' matches. They believed that they could outperform the 401(k) in non-qualified investments with fewer strings attached.

Sam and Lisa did not look wealthy, and at the time they came to see me, they were still dependent upon their jobs. With an average home and average cars, they looked like the picture of the average family in their new suburban neighborhood. But Sam and Lisa were anything but average. They had invested time in increasing their fiscal literacy. They had formed a plan and had clearly defined goals. They had assembled a team of experts to help them execute their plan, and they were clearly on the path to their financial freedom date.

> *Financial freedom date: The date when we will finally be doing what we want to do with our time. This date is moved up as we protect and optimize our wealth, manage our cash flow, and increase our fiscal literacy.*
>
> ~Daniel C. Goodwin

Fiscal Literacy Points

- Manage cash flow.
- Create a reserve account.
- Pay yourself first.
- Say "no" to dumb debt.
- Set goals.

Cash Flow Management - Profit & Loss
You can also download a copy of this worksheet at www.WeRetireWell.com.

Total Monthly Gross Income	**$____________**
- Taxes, Health Ins. & Other Payroll Deductions	$_________
- Savings, 401K, etc.	$_________
= Total Monthly 'Spendable' Income	**$____________**

Housing Expenses	Monthly Payments
Rent or Mtg.	$_________
Utilities	$_________
Insurance (set $ aside each month if paid annually)	$_________
Repairs (set $ aside for future expenses)	$_________
Taxes (set $ aside if paid annually)	$_________
= Total	**$_________**

Car Expenses	
Loan Payment(s)	$_________
Gas	$_________
Insurance (set $ aside if paid annually)	$_________
Maintenance & Repairs (set $ aside for future expenses)	$_________
= **Total**	**$_________**

Debts	
Creditor #1____________ Balance_________	$_________
Creditor #2____________ Balance_________	$_________
Creditor #3____________ Balance_________	$_________
Creditor #4____________ Balance_________	$_________
(figure more on back if needed)	
= **Total**	**$_________**

Miscellaneous	
(Set $ aside each month for annual expenses, such as Ins.)	
Church Tithes & Offerings	$________
Other Charitable Contributions	$________
Groceries, Lunches, Meals Out	$________
Childcare	$________
School Tuition/Supplies	$________
Medical Bills and Co-Pays	$________
Prescription Medicines	$________
Pet Supplies & Vet Exams	$________
Entertainment, Cable, Video Rentals	$________
Club Dues (Homeowner's Assoc., Fitness, etc...)	$________
Newspaper, Magazine Subscriptions	$________
Clothing	$________
Haircuts	$________
Gifts	$________
Cash	$________
Other (continue on back if needed)	$________
= **Total**	**$**________

Monthly Expense Totals	
Housing	$________
Car	$________
Debts	$________
Miscellaneous	$________
= **Total Expenses**	**$**________

Monthly Surplus or Shortage	**$**____________
(Total Spendable Income *minus* Total Expenses)	

Chapter Three

The Five Ways to Profit from Real Estate

Investment: an asset held to have some recurring or capital gains; an asset that is expected to give returns without any work on the asset per se. Some call this money that works for you.

Investing in real estate for passive income is one of the single best ways that you and I can grow our wealth the fastest. Passive income moves each of us closer to our financial freedom date, the date when we will be doing what we want to do with our time. Investing in real estate may not be suitable for everyone; however, far too many people make poor excuses: "I'm too old." "I'm too young." "It's too complicated." "Real estate is risky." "I don't have enough money to invest in real estate." "I invest in mutual funds." "I just don't have the time" "Too many people are in that racket." "I would not know where to start."

"The best deals are already taken." And the list goes on.

Real Estate Investing is Smart Investing

If you truly want to reach your financial freedom date while you are still living, the only way to do so is by replacing your current income. The fact is that you and I will need income for the remainder of our lives. Most people hope that their savings will one day get them to their destination; but I for one do not want to be caught staring at the mirage this concept conjures up, and neither do you. Saving is important and is a required part of your plan; however saving alone is a losing proposition. *You have to learn how to invest.* You have to challenge your fears, increase your fiscal literacy, and train or retrain your brain if you have fears about investing and real estate. Allow me to remind you of this: the main purpose of saving is to accumulate money to invest and to replenish your reserve fund as covered in chapter two of this book.

For example: If you needed one million dollars for retirement, and were able to save five hundred dollars per month, and could average an 8 percent return on your investment, you would find that in twenty-five years of savings you would not have even one-half of the million dollars you set out to save. Moreover, in twenty-five years, the money you managed to save would be worth about 40 percent of its original value due to inflation. You might have to think about marrying someone with money or moving in with your kids. How many people do you really know who have created wealth by saving? Not many, I'll bet. People create equity and wealth with real estate and investments. Real estate creates wealth faster than other investments because the invested money controls a much larger asset due to leverage.

In looking at leverage, let's consider that you use $50,000 of your own money to purchase a commercial building worth $250,000. You are using a 20 percent down payment to control 100 percent of a commercial property or rental home. Many people use leverage when buying their home without even realizing their own brilliance! Your situation will soon improve with depreciation. After you purchase the building, a certain percentage will be depreciable. If you are entitled to 3 percent depreciation on the $250,000 building per year, you will have a $7,500 tax write-off. If you are being taxed at a 30 percent rate it will yield a direct savings of $2,250. Your savings are equal to a 4.5 percent return on your original investment of $55,000 just in the depreciation on the property.

In addition you get the appreciation on the full amount of $250,000. So if the building goes up in value by 5 percent, you will have made $12,500 in addition to the $2,250. Your first year internal rate of return, not counting the value of your amortization or cash flow, would be 30 percent. If you create $10,000 in positive cash flow and your loan balance goes down by $4,000 per year, you could calculate a first-year value on the equity you invested of 58 percent. In short, leverage and tax-favored depreciation are preferred methods of the wealthy, who understand how money really works inside real estate investments.

For the record, I am not a self-proclaimed real estate guru or someone who thinks real estate is the holy grail of all investments, and I am keenly aware that people do lose money in real estate and many other kinds of investments. Real estate is just one component of my portfolio, albeit the most important one. Real estate has done far more to bring quantum leaps to the balance sheets of my family and millions of other families than any other sort of investment—bar none.

My family and I live in The Woodlands, Texas, a suburb of Houston. In Harris County, which surrounds Houston, there are over 107,000 millionaires. In Los Angeles County, California, there are more than twice as many millionaires as in Houston. It has been estimated that there are more than 5 million millionaires in America at this time. While it is difficult to determine the source for this wealth, one study found that real estate contributed to as much as 50 percent of these individual's first million dollars. I believe there is more opportunity in real estate in America than ever before. America's population stands at 300 million and is expected to exceed 400 million sometime before 2050. Real estate will be the basis for a staggering amount of all new wealth created as demand for housing, apartments, commercial buildings, retail centers, and vacation properties increases.

A whole new generation, called the echo boom generation, is set to follow the baby boomers. The echo boomers, primarily the children of baby boomers, were born between 1980 and 1994. They represent more than 70 million consumers in the U.S. economy and have fueled the rise of megatrends such as MySpace, YouTube, Facebook, text messaging, and many other popular phenomena. This generation, along with the 1.5 million new immigrants arriving every year, will create a new wave of demand for virtually every type of real estate investment. You need to be educated and ready to move on real estate opportunities, as they will be most abundant in the years to come. Forget about this week's headlines and the fear mongering that the newswires feed on; after all, negative news is what sells the most TV time. One thing is certain in any economy: real estate is here to stay, hence the term *real estate*.

Yes, markets will rise and fall in real estate and in every other investment, but the ebb and flow of the markets and economy are where our opportunities are found. You should be excited when markets are down because down markets will likely provide buying opportunities. When the markets are up, count your blessings and hold on. Real estate is a long-term play and not the game for day traders, who celebrate one day and seek counseling the next. I know the media wants you and me to think the sky is always falling; but take their reports with a grain of salt and remember that there are plenty of people out there who are making money while others are reaching for the panic button. I recommend this site to all of my friends: www.positiveeconomicnews.com. I get e-mails every day from this service that help me counterbalance the negative economic news that seems to creep into all of our lives one way or another. Consider this statement from Andrew Carnegie: "More money has been made in real estate than in all industrial investments combined."

Today, far too many portfolios are structured with too little emphasis on real estate. I have heard financial advisors and mutual fund sellers tell clients that their homes represent the real estate allocation in their portfolios and that the rest of their money should be diversified into mutual funds. While this may be suitable advice for a very few people, it would hardly qualify as good advice for most Americans. I believe this advice benefits the mutual fund sellers the most, and right now they are not my highest priority—my family is.

Many people avoid real estate because it sounds too time-consuming, too risky, and too difficult to learn, especially when compared to mutual funds. After all, the financial advisor offers a vehicle that allows you to merely transfer funds and walk away. The trouble in doing this is that we also give away control of our money, tax advantages, leverage opportunities, and the chance to increase our fiscal literacy by taking charge of our own financial futures with real estate and other more productive investments. Most people, if given the choice and education, would prefer to build wealth quickly rather than slowly, which real estate investing supports. Most people simply lack the knowledge, tools, and education to use leverage, other people's money, and the favored benefits of our tax code, even though they would prefer to do so. Most people know, even if they are not real estate investors, that more money and passive income are made (and more quickly) in real estate than in all other investments.

I have had people tell me that they are safe in their CDs and mutual funds. I believe there is a kernel of truth to their statements, but I do not believe people are as safe as they might think. In most economic environments, people are aware that CDs struggle to keep pace with inflation; however, they forget that the forecasted inflation numbers, called *core inflation*, strips out food and energy costs. I don't know about you, but my family is definitely paying more these days in food, and filling up at the pump has been a killer. If you add back these real cost increases, *real* inflation is much higher than the government's posted figures for core inflation.

Let's look at an example:

We have a $50,000 CD earning 5 percent interest. After the first year, our CD has earned $2500 in interest. Assuming a 30 percent tax bracket, we pay $750 in taxes on our $2500 in interest. The difference we get to keep is $1,750 in earned in come. Adding $1,750 to our original investment gives us a net cash amount of $51,750. But here's the problem – inflation has grown at a rate of 4 percent meaning our money is worth 4 percent less today than it was a year ago. That means our $51,750 today is equivalent to $49,680 last year.

$50,000 @ 5%	*Value of Certificate of Deposit (CD)*
$2,500	*Earned interest on CD*
$2,500 x 30%	*Earned interest multiplied by tax bracket*
$750	*Taxes paid on earned interest*
$1,750	*Net interest income after taxes*
$51,750 x 4%	*Total net investment multiplied by inflation rate*
$2,070	*Loss represented by adjustment due to inflation*
$49,680	*Adjusted investment value after interest and inflation*

We've lost money by investing! Tell me again how we get ahead like this?

How Banks Work

Banks take our money in through the front door and lend it out through the back. They pay us 4 to 5 percent interest on our CDs, and then they take the money we just gave them and lend it to our neighbors at 7 to 8 percent interest. They earn a little spread on every dollar that passes through the bank. Can a bank earn money on a little spread of 3 to 4 percent? I have a hint for you: the banks are not getting rich on free checking!

In case you haven't noticed, banks are not non-profits. I seem to see banks popping up everywhere and buying some of the most valuable real estate in our marketplaces. These guys have it down. They make piles of cash by lending out someone else's money and earn a spread (or *arbitrage*, as it is known in the banking world). They are capitalizing on some of the very best real estate in the country with your money and mine. You have to love the genius in this! The banks want to invest in real estate and other investments, but they want us to deposit our money with them where it is "safe." But is it really safe? Well, probably. But you might be surprised to know that for every dollar FDIC insures, only about eight cents is in real cash reserves. That's comforting, no?

That being said, I must acknowledge that I also have money in banks. My money is there for immediate cash reserves and emergencies, but I don't consider it to be invested. My money is positioned in banks to show some liquidity to my banker, who will feel more comfortable loaning money to me if he can see that I could weather a storm. Money in the bank can serve a strategic purpose as cash reserves, but please do not feel like you are invested if you are trying to build wealth in CDs.

Where Do You Start?

In light of the national real estate collapse opportunities in this investment sector may be better now than ever before. Like in the game of Monopoly, most people like to cut their teeth with just one rental home, then move up to several rental homes or a multi-family property, and then on to commercial property. I want to encourage you to consider a few things before you immediately go down the default path of starting with single-family rental homes. First consider how much cash you (or perhaps you and a partner) can assemble. You might be in a position to buy a much larger property than you thought or even a commercial building.

To illustrate, I'll tell you about one of my early real estate investments. I have a close friend, Clint, whom I have known for over ten years. Our families are also close, and I was asked to be the godfather to their first-born son, which I accepted. Because our trust, confidence, and respect for one anther sit on a firm foundation, I was most comfortable going into a partnership with my friend.

Clint's family was in the real estate business in the Texas hill country and had come across a commercial building for sale in a very nice downtown area. The building had multiple suites, but only a few of them were leased to businesses. We felt confident that, with a few minor improvements, we could lease the remainder of the spaces. Most of the other real estate investors in the area had overlooked this property because they believed it lacked potential. Clint and I decided to buy the building and in three years were able to accomplish a great deal.

We purchased the property was $350,000. We obtained an 80 percent loan through a local bank, paying the remaining 20 percent as our downpayment, a total of $70,000 out -of-pocket. Within three months, we were able to make minor improvements to the available spaces and become fully leased. Our annual rents exceeded our bank payments, taxes, insurance, and repair reserves by $24,000. With costs and profits divided between the two of us, Clint and I were able to experience a 34% return on investment just in the first year.

$70,000	*20% downpayment on bank loan*
$24,000	*First year positive cash flow*
34%	*First year cash on cash return*

How many CDs or mutual funds do you know of that offer a 34% return on investment? In addition, we also were able to depreciate the value of our building according to an IRS-approved schedule that our CPA and tax attorney monitored. This gave us each a way to avoid much of the income tax on our earnings.

During the period that we owned the building, we had two other attractive features working for us. First, the loan balance went down every month as we made our payments, and second, the building was appreciating nicely. In addition, we implemented two rent increases during the time we owned the building, improving our cash flow further as well as our internal rate of return (IRR). When Clint and I sold the building three years later for $450,000, we calculated the following investment returns:

$450,000	*Sales price*
-$270,000	*Loan payoff*
-$20,000	*Closing costs and commissions*
=$160,000	*Profit from appreciation after sale*
-$70,000	*Initial out-of-pocket investment*
+$72,000	*Three years of profit from rental income*
+$160,000	*Profit from appreciation after sale*
=$162,000	*Total gross profit*

$162,000 Profit ÷ $70,000 Down Payment = 231% Return on Investment after three years!

This probably sounds too good to be true to those who have no experience investing in real estate. Most people are unaware of how leverage and the tax code really work in favor of the real estate investor; they think returns in the 30 to 100 percent range are unobtainable. Rates of return like this, along with favored tax benefits, are not even remotely realistic with mutual funds as they employ no leverage in their investments and, in my opinion, involve much more risk.

Here is a thought for you: investing in real estate is not a new idea. The market for single-family homes is most crowded because just about any bozo can buy one of these properties. Scores of people make millions pedaling books and DVDs on "making a fortune in real estate." Most of this so-called education directs people to start with low-priced homes and rent them out or try to flip them. They also teach people to hang around courthouses and look for destitute homeowners who are under financial duress and then circle like sharks in the water to feed on these struggling homeowners. As you might expect, the success stories of these peddlers are built around the needle-in-the-haystack examples. Few people are ever able to duplicate the results that are represented in these books and seminars, but there is a better way to make money in real estate. Consider a niche where all of the real estate amateurs are afraid to go: commercial income-producing properties that generate a positive cash flow.

What I like about commercial real estate is that investors do not have to compete with the scores of amateurs who have just read a book, attended a seminar, or joined a real estate coaching program and are now out looking for their first real estate gig. This sort of amateur investing reminds me of the time that I fished a segment of a river during a short salmon season in Idaho. The river was so crowded with fishermen that we felt like we were almost shoulder to shoulder. We called it "combat fishing." Now I call hunting for single-family rental home deals the same thing. I can acknowledge that there is money to be made in this gambit, but I like better results and better returns at a faster pace. I go commercial.

In commercial, you can operate in a space above all of the novice wannabes but below the institutional firms that dominate the commercial markets; you do this by focusing on commercial income-producing properties priced between two hundred thousand and one million dollars.

My portfolio of real estate investments now includes site plans for thirty-two thousand square feet of prime retail space and the remaining parcels of a 2,400-acre private hunting ranch in Junction, Texas. Projects that are in the planning phase include more than eighty thousand square feet of prime medical and professional office space and another ranch development property. These projects total well over twenty million dollars and became possible as a result of utilizing some very astute real estate professionals, tax advantages, and leverage.

In the interest of full disclosure, I must note that I have made real estate investments that were nowhere near as profitable as the example I described earlier, while others produced even better returns. I broke even on five properties because the market was soft and I sold too soon. Every deal you do is not going to be a slam dunk, but you have to be in the game if you want the bigger returns. I get comfortable when I can estimate that my worst case is breaking even. To estimate your return on investment and your internal rate of return you must do a mock proforma before you commit to purchasing the property. I recommend using software from planEASe, which you can find at www.planEASe.com. PlanEASe is a desktop software program that analyzes the cash flow of commercial real estate investments, developments, leases, exchanges, loans, and the like, along with creating discounted cash flow measures like internal rate of return and the cumulative rate of return over time. The program computes and shows ratios such as cash-on-cash return, cap rate, debt coverage ratio, and more, all with beautiful reports and graphs.

If you have no experience as a real estate investor, I recommend that you start your education with *The Millionaire Real Estate Investor* by Gary Keller. Devour this book and others like it. Ask several real estate brokers to show you active commercial properties for sale before you line your sights up to buy a property. The analysis software will become easier to understand as you work with real examples, and the information on the commercial listing sheets should fit right into the analysis software from planEASe.

Please remember that as a novice you might initially lack the experience and sophistication to adequately analyze the date, leases, financing, and other relevant factors when buying a commercial property. I cannot stress enough that you should seek out competent professional advice. I am a firm believer in paying professionals such as tax attorneys, CPAs, and other advisors and consultants for their time and expertise. I consider it valuable leverage. For example, to evaluate my legal documents, I am able to utilize the many years of education and experience that my attorney possesses for a reasonable, one-time fee. The same is true for my CPA. Let the professionals do what they do; leverage their expertise for your investments. I once paid a utility consultant several thousand dollars for his time, expertise, and advice in solving a difficult utility issue. Over time the investment proved to be worth many times the cost of his advice. In the process, I made a lifetime friend who became a mentor to me. Priceless! Your CPA and tax attorney can set up the required entities that you will need to purchase commercial real estate such as a Limited Liability Partnership (LLP), which usually is preferable to an LLC and other entity, for real estate investments. *Do not* do this on your own as each state has individual considerations and tax code requirements on which your tax professional can provide appropriate advice.

Partners

Consider someone whom you would be comfortable being partners with. I have two such partners, whom I would trust with anything, including my money and my family; these are the sort of people worth considering. While most people speak out against partnerships I am a believer in pooling resources that can be both financial and intellectual assets. One of my partners has a construction engineering degree from Texas A&M. We work great together because I am the numbers and money partner and he is the expert on buildings and construction. We pool our funds and have brought in other partners for bigger projects. When a project is completed, like our commercial building that we sold for $450,000, we move on to larger projects such as shopping centers, commercial buildings, office space, and ranch subdivisions.

If you decide to start with a rental home, consider offering the rental on a short-term basis such as three to six months and offer the property fully furnished. I have found that in the community where I live that this is a much underserved market. With shorter-term leases you can expect more vacancy, but even if you stay rented only 75 percent of the time on a short-term lease versus 90 percent of the time on a one-year or longer lease, you can more than make up the ground with the much higher rents that short-term tenants are happy to pay. On one property I looked at the market for a one-year lease was $1,200 per month where a short-term furnished unit would go for $1,800 per month. With a 75 percent occupancy rate, $1,800 per month amounts to $16,200 per year in rent, while $1,200 dollars per month with a 90 percent occupancy rate brings in only $13,200.

This small strategy alone could improve your ROI by 20 percent, and you won't have to go combat fishing with all of the other rental home investors. A short-term furnished rental property can be an excellent way to begin as a real estate investor if you lack the confidence to begin with commercial property.

Remember that you will likely find more attractive terms on longer fixed rates with up to four rental homes using your local mortgage professional because rental homes are eligible as mortgage products while commercial buildings are not. Better financing terms will translate to better investment returns. Commercial properties have to be financed with local banks or commercial lenders, and the terms always require more money down and shorter fixed-rate periods. If you are buying a rental home or condo, be advised that your mortgage loan officer will not be able to lend to an LLP or LLC; mortgage loans are made to individuals and not entities.

Individual Retirement Accounts

Did you know that it is perfectly legal to use your IRA to purchase investment real estate? For years, banks and brokerage firms have lobbied to convince us that our IRA money can only be invested in the mutual funds and bonds that they are selling. Baloney! How many Americans would be better off investing their IRAs in real estate (at least partially), where leverage, depreciation, and tax-favored treatment of gains could be harnessed? Most people simply have no idea that the lazy, idle dollars trapped in their IRAs could be the money they invest in real estate. In fact, anyone with an IRA, Education IRA, Keogh plan, Savings Incentive Match Plan (SIMPLE), or Simplified Employee Pension (SEP) can take control of their funds and how they are invested. Americans have had the ability to do this for decades, but very few actually do.

Why is it that close to one hundred million Americans have IRAs, Keoghs, or SEP accounts of some sort but less that 1 percent of them take advantage of the ability to invest this money in real estate? In two words: *fiscal literacy*. Instead, like drones we are programmed by the voice of the large investment houses, running Super Bowl ads at two million dollars a pop, to believe that they and their mutual funds are the answer to our futures. Friend, if you are raking it in with this as your plan, then I would advise you to stay the course. I can say this easily because I know that you are not raking it in with your IRA and the mutual funds your IRA likely contains. I know you are not using the leverage and tax-favored benefits that the IRS affords real estate.

If you are serious about learning how to use your IRA to buy real estate, then buy *IRA Wealth* by Patrick W. Rice. Rice has written a complete and comprehensive guide to investing in real estate with your IRA. You will need a custodian; and the rules for using your IRA are etched in stone, so make sure that you educate yourself first and proceed as soon as you have clarity about the process. The custodian firms that offer these services have great training resources, and you can become an expert on the subject by investing just a couple days of your time.

Investing the REIT Way

Some people may benefit from real estate exposure to their mix of investments with a Real Estate Investment Trust (REIT). REITs may be suitable for those who want to invest in real estate but do not want to own real estate outright because of the risk of negative cash flow. Think of a REIT as a real estate fund managed by internal partners. You buy an interest in the REIT with the expectation of dividends and appreciation. There is little possibility of negative cash flow, which you might have if you own a rental property that sits vacant for a period of time. While I believe that most people would benefit from more exposure to real estate investments, I understand that buying commercial properties and rental homes is not a suitable activity for everyone. My single, seventy-year-old mother, for example, would have no business buying a commercial building, although another seventy-year-old might. But my mother could own shares in a REIT and gain exposure to a real estate vehicle that would probably be more suitable for her specific needs. REITs can be purchased through a qualified financial advisor. There are many types of REITs, specializing in many sectors of real estate. Work with someone knowledgeable, whom you trust and who has been screened according to the instructions in chapter 10.

While this may all sound daunting to the novice investor, you might be surprised at what you can accomplish when you have a clear vision and a plan. When you educate yourself, increase your fiscal literacy, and surround yourself with like-minded people, you can accomplish anything.

Be armed and ready for all of those people, including your loved ones, who will try to distract or dissuade you from your goals. They will say things like, "Come on now; be realistic. Investing is risky. You can't do that! What if this or that happens? Why don't you just do something safe like invest in CDs or mutual funds?" The truth is that most people who are stuck in mediocrity either despise, or are jealous of, those who rise above them. They would rather have your company in *their* comfort zone. Watching you succeed would remind them of their own lack of courage to try something new and to get a financial education. These will be the same folks saying later, when your investments have paid off, that you got lucky or that you came from money. Unfortunately, this is just human nature, so watch out. Be ready to say with a smile, “You know, staying in my comfort zone and never getting a financial education and doing things the way the masses do just never appealed to me that much.”

Fiscal Literacy Points

- Real estate utilizes leverage, the tax benefits of depreciation, and capital gains tax rates, which are lower than ordinary income tax.
- The opportunities in real estate are abundant, and demographics predict increased demand.
- Learn how to analyze a property with planEASe software and read the *Millionaire Real Estate Investor* by Gary Keller.

- Find a great partner and do not assume that you cannot start with commercial deals.
- Require commercial real estate agents to present properties and financial data to you. Ask them to provide a proforma. Listen.
- Consider your IRA as a source of investment funds.
- Seek out competent financial and legal advice from qualified and specialized advisors such as a CPA, tax attorney, and real estate attorney.
- CDs and mutual funds will not get you where you want to go fast enough, in large part, because they do not employ leverage.

Every day, you'll have opportunities to take chances and to work outside your safety net. Sure, it's a lot easier to stay in your comfort zone, but sometimes you have to take risks. When the risks pay off, that's when you reap the biggest rewards.

~ Donald Trump

Chapter Four

Meet Your New Best Friend—Your Mortgage!

In the continuing education (CE) classes that I have taught over the years to financial professionals, I commonly ask the attendees if they currently have mortgages. Most hands go up. Next, I will ask those who wish they *did not* have mortgages to keep their hands raised. Most hands stay up. Many people wish that their homes were paid off and they were mortgage-free. I believe this clearly reflects our common attitude and misunderstanding about mortgages and how they can be used to help us create significant wealth during our lifetimes. Remember that my attendees are often financial advisors, people who are supposed to have all the answers about investments and finance for their customers. It is not hard for me to imagine what kind of advice they are likely giving their clients. You have heard it a thousand times: "Pay your home off and max out your 401(k) in diversified mutual funds." The mantra of the masses. Let me show you why I believe traditional mainstream financial planning has failed millions of Americans who need every legal advantage that is available to them, including optimizing their mortgages.

Paying Off a Mortgage vs. Building Wealth

Many people consider aggressive methods such as fifteen-year mortgages, bi-weekly payments, and sending extra money to their mortgage companies each month because they know that over the life of a thirty-year loan they will pay back in interest two to three times the original loan amount. To save money on interest it seems logical to make bigger down payments or extra principal payments, however most people never understand the tax ramifications and lost opportunity costs of this flawed thinking. Saving money is not the same as building wealth. Or, said differently, paying off debt may not have as important an effect on your retirement as accumulating assets. There is a big difference, and millions of Americans are getting this wrong every day.

Many people feel paying off their home is the best use of their cash. The wealthy believe otherwise.

Paying Off a Mortgage	Building Wealth
• $1,580 monthly note on a $250,000 mortgage	• $1,580 monthly contribution to an investment account
• Fixed-rate thirty-year mortgage at 6.5 percent	• Conservative, long-term rate of return at 8 percent
• After thirty years with 4 percent appreciation of the home:	• After thirty years with compounding interest:
$810,000	**$2,319,677**

As the example above proves, there is a tremendous difference between paying off a mortgage and building wealth. When we borrow at 6.5 percent, we really pay 4.5 percent if we are taxed at 30 percent. This is because we deduct our mortgage interest. If we can borrow at a net cost of 4.5 percent with a simple interest mortgage and earn at a rate of 4.5 percent or better in a compounding environment, we can create what bankers call arbitrage. Arbitrage is the lifeblood of every financial institution. Let's say that, as I am writing this, you put your money in a bank; they might pay you 4 to 5 percent. The bank will then lend that money to your neighbor at 7 to 8 percent. This little spread of borrowing at 4 to 5 percent and earning at 7 to 8 percent makes banks millions. When we pay off or pay down our mortgages, we give our arbitrage opportunity away. This is usually because of a lack of fiscal literacy.

Stay with me here because this is one of the most important chapters in the book. I want every reader to understand this simple money concept, which millions of Americans overlook. Remember these are the same millions of Americans who need every ounce of opportunity available to them as they struggle to reach their retirement goals and financial freedom dates, when they will finally be doing what they want with their time.

Have you ever gone to the store to buy a drill? Did you really want a drill, or did you want what a drill could do for you—make a hole? No one wants a mortgage itself; a mortgage is just a sheet of paper with words on it. Just like the drill, it's what the mortgage can *do* for you in creating arbitrage that is important. Arbitrage is borrowing at one rate and earning at another. Most Americans miss this because they do not understand the tax-advantaged component of deductible interest and what harnessing arbitrage can do for a family in the creation of wealth.

Let's look at another example of mortgage arbitrage where one might have the choice in paying down or paying off their mortgage.

Question: *Can I do well borrowing money at 7 percent and then earning 8 percent?*

Answer: First, you need to calculate the net interest paid on a loan. Because interest paid is tax deductible, you want to be certain you are using the effective net rate. Assuming a 30 percent tax bracket, the actual net interest paid on a 7 percent loan is 4.9 percent and the calculations would be as follows:

$200,000 borrowed on interest-only mortgage at 7% with an assumed tax bracket of 30%

Effective net borrowing rate due to mortgage tax adjustment: 4.9%

$200,000 × 4.9% = $9,800 out of pocket
(cost of borrowing per year)

$9,800 × 30 years = **$294,000**
(Total cost of borrowing)

$200,000 invested earning 8% with compounding interest for 30 years = **$2,012,531**

Difference = $1,718,531

Therefore, if you were to take $200,000 and invest it at 8% while making interest-only payments on a 30 year mortgage as opposed to paying cash for your property, you would stand to gain over $1.7 million dollars even before appreciation of the property is added to the calculation. By not paying down or paying off a mortgage your money works much harder for you. The answer is YES!

Does it make sense for me to pay $294,000 in interest cost if it allows me the chance to earn over $2,000,000 with my money? The wealthy and fiscally literate believe it does. What would cost me more: borrowing $200,000 at a net rate of 4.9 percent or giving away my opportunity to earn 8 percent on $200,000 over thirty years?

It's just that simple. Read this again and think about the fact that most Americans never consider the opportunity cost of paying down or paying off their mortgages; they never realize that their money could grow much faster in investments.

If I borrowed $200,000 on my mortgage, paying 7 percent (net cost of 4.9 percent) and I grew my money at 7 percent, my $200,000 would have grown to over $1,500,000 in thirty years. Round my borrowing cost to $300,000, and my net would be over $1,200,000. Do the math and ask yourself again. Why am I in a hurry to mow down my mortgage? The wealthy have understood this for years. Why do so many middle class folks miss this one?

Let me ask you this: Is owning a home a long-term proposition for you? Could you use another one or two million dollars for your retirement and investment planning? Has anyone ever helped you look at the math on this issue? Are you missing the boat on this right now? If so, read on.

So, why do we view our mortgages as evil things that should be avoided or eliminated? I believe that our thinking about mortgages has been largely shaped over generations by our parents and grandparents, some of whom may have actually lived through the Great Depression and other times of economic hardship. Some of our parents or grandparents might even recall the period of time between 1925 and 1929, the Roaring Twenties, when the stock market was making epic gains. As we know, the bubble burst in 1929, and millions of Americans lost everything they had, including their homes.

At that time, banks had clauses in their agreements that allowed them to call mortgages due at any time and for any reason. Because Wall Street investors were running to the banks to cover margin calls as the stock market collapsed, banks began calling mortgages due on homeowners, most of whom were not even stock market investors. Most saw their home values fall 20 to 50 percent, and foreclosure was unavoidable because these homeowners lacked the liquidity to ride out the economic storm.

The stock market collapsed due to overvalued equities and a panic that resulted in a run on banks. Over five thousand banks failed, and millions of homeowners—out of work and unable to make their mortgage payments—were foreclosed upon. After the Great Depression, most reasoned that they should at least have their homes paid off so that if the economy collapsed again, the banks could not take their homes away.

In the years to follow, the government passed laws to regulate banks more heavily. The Fed is now quick to inject money into our system as it did in 1987, 2000, after 9/11, and during the credit crunch of 2008. Also the FDIC was created to insure banks. Still it's no wonder a distrust of banks and a fear of mortgages has become common with most Americans. In the 1950s and 1960s, families would throw mortgage-burning parties and celebrate making their very last mortgage payments. Our parents and grandparents had good reasons in their eyes to instruct us to pay down and pay off our mortgages; this was good judgment during their working years.

Today, however, you and I live in a much different environment than our parents and grandparents did, with a completely different set of rules and tax codes. We are not likely to hold the same jobs for thirty years, and we cannot depend on company pensions for our retirements. Our grandparents never had to learn how to invest because most Americans could simply plan to stay at their jobs for thirty years, pay off their homes, and retire with pensions and Social Security. Today things are radically different, so your financial strategies should be as well. It is not uncommon to have multiple careers, and employees often work for many different companies during their earning years. We move more often—some of us every four to six years—and we often have to change companies to advance our careers. We refinance our homes multiple times to restructure debt, remodel, and reset our rates. We are behind on our savings and retirement planning and are losing confidence in the American dream. We are not confident that we will be able to depend on Social Security, and we face many more pressures in corporate environments.

To make matters worse, most Americans drastically overpay unnecessary interest with their home mortgages *and* miss out on one of the most tax-advantaged financial strategies. Many Americans have no idea what effect an emphasis on paying off their mortgages instead of building wealth will have over time, especially on the value and quality of their retirements. Many Americans have no idea how mortgages can reduce their taxes, provide cash flow for investing, and mitigate the risk of foreclosure. Many Americans today are implementing financial strategies that were suitable for their parents and grandparents but that are poor choices for today. Many people make some of their most important financial decisions based on F.E.A.R.: false evidence appearing real.

Let's look at another basic example of how a mortgage can be an important tool utilizing the tax-favored treatment the IRS affords mortgages, along with the value of compounding over time. Consider two homeowners with very different views on mortgages and investing: Fiscal Frank and Fearsome Fred.

Fiscal Frank	**Fearsome Fred**
Current net worth: $300,000	Current net worth: $300,000
Buys a home for $300,000 Takes out a mortgage for $240,000 Puts $60,000 down Invests $240,000	**Buys a home for $300,000** Hates mortgages and is proud to be debt-free. Pulls all his resources together and pays cash for his home
Total assets: $540,000 $300,000 home and $240,000 in investments	**Total Assets: $300,000** $300,000 home and no debt
Net worth: $300,000	**Net worth: $300,000**

After twenty years, Fiscal Frank, who has carried an interest-only mortgage at 7 percent, has made mortgage payments totaling $336,000. Fearsome Fred has been most proud to tell everyone that he owns his home free and clear and that he has never made a single mortgage payment. Fearsome Fred never invested much time improving his fiscal literacy and knows little about the leverage and tax advantages that real estate offers. Fiscal Frank and Fearsome Fred live in the same neighborhood. Both need to build wealth for retirement planning and college funding. Both hope to be able to leave their current jobs one day. The neighborhood where they live has homes that have appreciated 4 percent per year on average over the 20 years. But Fiscal Frank has had two very large advantages over Fearsome Fred during the past twenty years: growth on his investment account averaging 8 percent and tax breaks from writing off his mortgage interest. Both now own their homes free and clear.

Let's look more closely to see how these two friends with very different views on money have done with their very different strategies.

	Fiscal Frank	Fearsome Fred
Home Value*:	$ 657,336	$ 657,336
(4% Appreciation)		
Tax Credits*:	$ 100,800	$ -
(30% Tax Bracket)		
Investments*:	$ 1,118,629	$ -
($240,000, 8% Compounded)*		
Cost of Mortgage Interest*:	$ (336,000)	$ -

	Fiscal Frank	Fearsome Fred
($240,000 x net interest rate)*		
Mortgage Payoff:	$ (240,000)	$ -
Net Worth*:	$ 1,300,765	$ 657,336
*After 20 Years		
Net Worth After 30 Years	$ 2,727,717	$ 970,017

An interview with Fearsome Fred might go something like this:

Interviewer: *So, Fred, tell me why you decided to pay cash for your home.*

Fred: Well, I figured that what I wanted was to own a home free and clear. My granddad told me that I should pay my mortgage off as soon as possible, and look at all of the interest I saved!

Interviewer: *I see you saved several hundred thousand dollars in interest charges that your neighbor Frank had to pay. But what about your tax write-offs?*

Fred: You know, I never agreed with the notion of a tax deduction. In my eyes, I would be spending a dollar to save thirty cents. I would rather get the debt out of the way. That's what I hear the financial guys on the radio and TV say.

Interviewer: *But what about the money you used to pay off your home? Wouldn't you have been better off investing some of that money?*

Fred: My home is my investment! My dad's home is paid off, and so is his dad's. They have done OK, and so have I!

Interviewer: *Fred, did you know that Frank came out ahead of you by close to $650,000 by investing most of his money, averaging only 8 percent returns, while he sheltered his income with tax breaks?*

Fred: You know, I always knew that guy Frank was crooked somehow. I'll bet he cheated some kind of way. So, are we done here? I have some buddies coming over to watch the game.

Interviewer: *Sure, Fred. Just one last point: $2,681 per month.*

Fred: What do you mean?

Interviewer: *Fred, for the twenty years that you've lived in your home, if you could had saved $2,681 per month through investments, tax deductions and growth without having to reach into your pocket to find the money would you have wanted to do that? $2,681 every month for 240 months equals $643,440 (difference in wealth between Frank and Fred)*

Fred: Sure, but it sounds too good to be true.

Sometimes when you look at the compounding of money over time, it can seem too good to be true. But when we discuss money, we're talking about numbers. Money is in numbers, and numbers reflect math. Math and numbers are absolute without variance. There are no gray areas; the numbers either compute or they don't. If you ever think that the power of compounding looks too good to be true, consider a quote from on of the greatest minds of our time.

> *The most powerful force in the universe is the power of compound interest.*
>
> ~ Albert Einstein

Consider this question: can you average 8 percent on your money over time? Ask any financial planner for ten to one-hundred-year data on the Dow Jones Industrial average, the S&P, or any other index and look at the numbers for yourself. I like real estate, private placement partnerships, and principal protected-paper assets with which I would be very disappointed if I averaged anywhere close to 10 percent. Looking at long-term figures with an 8 percent average rate of return runs toward the ultraconservative view, and I would welcome any argument to the contrary. Also, consider that the math shows that I could borrow on a mortgage at 6 percent and only earn at 6 percent and *still* come out far ahead over time!

What if I borrowed on a home loan at 8 percent and only earned 6 percent with my money? Most would think this would get you nowhere fast, but would they be right?

Borrow: $100,000 (mortgage) at 8%	**Invest: $100,000 earning 6%**
25 percent tax bracket (net cost: 6%)	
Interest: $500 per month ($6,000 per year)	Compounding
Interest cost over thirty years	Thirty years to grow
Total interest cost: $180,000	Total value: $574,347
Net gain by borrowing 100K at *8% and earning at 6% = $394,349	

Let's be honest here: if I told you that you could borrow at 8 percent, earn at 6 percent, and make money doing it, you would never have believed me unless you saw the math, right?

What if you borrowed on a home loan at 6 percent, deducted your interest, and earned 10 percent on your investments over thirty years? If you applied the same principal to $250,000, your net positive difference would be over $4,000,000.

Do you want to see the math?

Borrow: $250,000 (mortgage) at 6%	**Invest: $250,000 earning 10%**
30 percent tax bracket (net cost: 4.2 percent)	
Interest: $875 per month ($10,500 per year)	Compounding at 10 percent
Interest cost over thirty years	Thirty years to grow
Total interest cost: $315,000	Total value: $4,362,350
Net Gain by borrowing 250K at 6% and earning at 10% = $4,047,350	

Today, information, education, and knowledge are the tools of the wealthy. Now more than ever, there is no excuse for not using your single largest asset (your home) as a wealth-creation tool. Today there is no place for Great Depression thinking or fear regarding your mortgage. Eric Tyson, national syndicate writer and author of *Let's Get Real About Money!*, writes, "There can be advantages to not paying all cash for a home and taking out a mortgage if you have investment opportunities." We all have investment opportunities. The trouble is most people only know about CDs, stocks, or mutual funds, where the risk can be high or the return can be low. Most people are not aware of the safer, more liquid investments of the wealthy. The chapters to come in this book will teach you how to find investment opportunities that emphasize safety, rate of return, liquidity, and tax efficiency. You would not stuff your money in a mattress or bury it in a can in your backyard, would you? What is the difference between stuffing money in a mattress and stuffing it inside the bricks and mortar of our homes?

We may feel safer when our homes are paid off, but the wealthy are not confused on this point. They have a different definition of being debt-free than most Americans do. *The wealthy consider themselves debt-free when they have the liquid wealth on their balance sheets to pay their homes off anytime they might want to, and they understand mortgages are what can get them there the fastest.* They choose not to tie up large sums of cash inside homes that would eliminate tax benefits and offer zero return on equity. By having cash available for emergencies and investment opportunities, most homeowners are better off than if their equity is tied up in their residences.

The irony is that many people pay their homes off because they believe it to be a conservative move, while in fact the opposite is true. What if they need the money? I have news for you: banks do not lend money to those who are unemployed or who cannot prove sufficient income. Unfortunately, too many people find this out in their times of need when they are experiencing sickness, unemployment, divorce, or economic hardship of some sort. What many people don't realize is that even if they've consistently been making double mortgage payments for five years in a row, the bank still will not work with them. If they suddenly experience a financial setback, the bank will not care. People can go to the bank and plead their cases: "I've been paying my mortgage in advance for years. How about if I just skip my mortgage payments for a few months?" They would all get the same answer: "Sorry, we just cannot help you! Your next payment is due." Banks just don't work in a way that will allow them to change your payment structure after you have closed. If your home is worth three hundred thousand dollars and you only owe fifty thousand, guess what? Your next payment will still be due on the first of the month—*period!*

Beginning in 2007 and 2008, Americans have watched the housing market drop dramatically in value due to overbuilding, overvaluing, and the subsequent credit and subprime crises. Across America hundreds of thousands of home are being foreclosed upon just as in the 1980s during the savings and loan crisis. Those who escape foreclosure are often so fully leveraged that the banks see more risk for themselves in foreclosure than in waiting for those particular homeowners to recover.

As a homeowner pays down his or her mortgage, risk is transferred from the bank to the homeowner. When the mortgage balance is high, the bank carries the most risk. If I am a banker who has to foreclose on fifty homes, I look for the ones that have the most equity, and I foreclose on those first. If you have little to no equity, I (the banker) am more likely to invite you into the bank and put my arm around you to let you know how much I care. Banks care, all right—they care about themselves. They do not want houses back on their balance sheets, and they will do anything they can do to help you through your tough time if you have little equity in your home. They'll send the foreclosure notice to your neighbor who has his home almost paid off. Can you blame them?

A bank is a place where they lend you an umbrella in fair weather and ask for it back when it begins to rain.

~ Robert Frost

Think the equity in your home is guaranteed and always safe? Try asking people in California who saw their homes destroyed in a forest fire, earthquake, or mudslide. Ask those in Iowa and Missouri whose homes were flooded as the Mississippi crested its banks and flooded their towns. Or how about those in New Orleans after Hurricane Katrina, or Florida after Hurricane Andrew? Ask those who have had business failures, layoffs, divorces, illnesses, or special needs children. Ask them how easy it was to get equity back out of their homes when they needed it.

Does home equity have any rate of return? In a word: NO! Your home will go up or down in value regardless of how you have it financed. Think about it: Pick any street in America in any market during any year. If you have two homes side by side and all things are equal, will the homeowner who paid cash have any greater increase or decrease in the value of his home than the owner who financed with a mortgage? Of course not! We get confused and think that the money that we pay into our homes is generating a rate of return. It's not the equity that goes up or down; it's the real estate asset that goes up or down. And that has nothing to do with us paying cash or financing. Since that is the case, why not have our cake and eat it too? Why not gain in the appreciation of our homes and our money when we keep our money invested outside of our home?

When we focus on building wealth instead of just paying off our mortgages, we create a harmony of tax benefits, arbitrage, compounding, and leverage that far overshadows any benefits of owning our homes free and clear. One day, you will be able to write a check and wipe out your home loan in one stroke if you ever wake up one day and decide you want it gone. You will just be doing it sooner and with more of the government's money than if you had proceeded down the default path of most Americans—those who do not understand or refuse to listen to simple and sound financial logic. Many insist that their granddads' way must be right; that's all they want to hear. Some people even attempt to impress me by letting me know that they have paid, or could pay off, their homes. I usually just let it go. I am always far more impressed when I meet someone who has invested in fiscal literacy over home equity. It disappoints me to know that most Americans and their financial advisors have no way to quantify and analyze mortgages as a wealth-creation strategy that optimizes the value of compounding, tax advantages, leverage, and arbitrage.

Mortgages and Retirement

Most retirees are finding themselves paying through the nose in taxes with no shelters. Traditional financial planning has failed millions of Americans by advising them to pay off their mortgages and max out their 401(k) s. Unfortunately, millions of Americans are beginning to realize the tax implications of this flawed idea as they head into retirement. The kids have grown up and moved away. The mortgage is paid off; most of their money is in qualified plans; and now taxes are due. Many believe that, with baby boom trends, they will be facing higher tax rates in the future. Also, most are not confident the government will be able to provide Social Security benefits.

The more astute retirees, those with wise financial advisors or who have invested time in increasing their fiscal literacy, are learning advanced concepts whereby in retirement mortgages can be their friends and not their foes. A mortgage that one's cash flow could easily support may offset all or a portion of qualified plan withdrawals. This strategy effectively gives retirees the opportunity to access a portion of the qualified plans tax-free. Moreover, their money remains invested, earning income in secure, liquid investments. Better planning equals more discretionary income in retirement.

I consider home equity to be sacred. When we separate it from home, it should be to build wealth, *not* to consume it. Home equity should be invested wisely and not aggressively. *Home equity is best invested in safe, conservative investment vehicles. Tax favored, principal-protected, safer investments are ideal.* You should make certain after reading this book that you are working with a professional team of advisors who share your beliefs about money and financial strategies. You *must* avoid rookie mutual fund sellers who have their companies' agendas shaping their advice. The final chapter of this book will give you the tools you need to make certain that you have the right team of advisors representing your interests and those of your family. You will find that when you have improved your fiscal literacy you will be more competent than most of the salespeople out there who are dispensing financial advice even though they are not investors themselves. Common conservative investment vehicles suitable for home equity may include: real estate, certain structured investments, insurance and annuities, IRAs with conservative allocations, and tax-free bonds.

Whom Do You Trust?

I have found over many years that financial advisors are all over the map on the subject of mortgages. Two very famous financial advisors, who are essentially entertainers, tell their television audiences that mortgages are essentially evil and that homeowners should pay off their mortgages as soon as possible. I must admit that this is the best advice for many of those who regularly view and listen to these shows. These TV entertainers are more often than not helping people who are dead broke and whose primary need is to get out of debt and stop the bleeding with their finances.

Let me take a moment now to offer you an important warning. *If your life is a financial mess, then what these entertainers have to say about your home mortgage is likely the best advice for you.* Avoid the strategies contained in this chapter. The strategies found here are for those who are already in control of their finances, who effectively manage their family P&Ls, and who can exercise discipline in investing.

A recent *Forbes* article states that someone who is in a higher tax bracket and who is investing for the future should ignore those who recommend an early payoff. High-net-worth families are not tuning in to radio and TV to figure out their finance and investment strategies. The fiscally literate are not drowning in debt, and they reject irrelevant advice about money from TV entertainers. They understand the tax code, leverage, arbitrage, and compounding, and they optimize every wealth strategy that they have control over.

You have to remember that there is good debt and bad debt. Exxon Mobil carries billions of dollars of debt on its balance sheet even though the company has the cash to wipe out all of its debt. Exxon Mobil and companies like it do this because they know they can pay bondholders 8 percent and then go into the marketplace and earn 15 to 20 percent with their cash. Their purpose is to create wealth for their shareholders, and I would say they have done a very good job regardless of how you may feel about Big Oil….. Corporate America and the wealthy understand the concept of arbitrage, and now you do too. Your mortgage is your new best friend. If your current mortgage needs to be analyzed, the final chapter of this book will show you how to select a professional financial planner who understands the concepts contained in this chapter and has the tools to help you evaluate a strategy for your own unique set of circumstances.

Fiscal Literacy Points

- Your mortgage is a wealth-creation tool.
- Arbitrage is made possible with a mortgage.
- Home equity has no rate of return.
- Mortgages support leverage, compounding, and tax savings.
- Contrary to common belief, paying off your home is not a conservative idea.
- The bank—not you—is safer, when your mortgage balance is low.
- Smart investors make safe investments with home equity dollars.
- You should be in control of your family P&L first.

Optimize your home mortgage now, and move toward your financial freedom date sooner rather than later.

~ Daniel C. Goodwin

Chapter Five

The IRS on a Diet

Picture yourself indoors on a gym basketball court. A two-gallon pail of water sits on a stool at the far end of the room. Your assignment is to pick up the pail water and then walk the length of the gym floor to dump your pail of water into a thousand-gallon storage tank. Once that's done, you are to return to the stool at the far end of the room to have your bucket refilled. You are to repeat the process until you have filled the storage tank. In your mind you have already calculated that it will require five hundred trips back and forth with your two-gallon bucket. You have also fixed some sort of timetable in your mind for the assignment. Your may even have given some thought to what you want to do after you finish at the gym since this all looks manageable to you and even a little fun. Eager and enthusiastic, you begin.

About eight steps into your first trip across the room, you feel something cool and wet running down your leg. You panic at first and wonder just what the heck that could be. You look down and see that it's the pail. The pail has holes in the bottom, and the water inside is leaking out the bottom, down your leg, and all over the gym floor. Your look to your instructors, and they wave you forward to continue your effort. You say, "Hey, this pail has holes!" They shrug and say, "We know, but it's the only pail we have. It's just going to take you longer."

What the heck is going on?, you ask yourself. You make your first trip to the storage tank, now with a little more hurry in your step because you realize that this could take a long time. You dump your first pail, and only about a cup of water dribbles into the large storage tank. Your contribution hardly even moistens the bottom of the tank. Evaporation scenarios start running through your mind. *Uh oh*, you think, *can I even do this? How long it is this going to take? Is there any way I can patch the holes at the bottom of the bucket and not lose so much water? Is patching the holes even allowed? Is there a better way?* You start to wonder if you are ever going to be able to leave this gym. You are up a creek without a paddle, as they say back home.

For many Americans, what is happening to the water in your bucket is exactly what is happening to their incomes. The bucket is the tax code, the water is your income, and the thousand-gallon storage tank is their retirement. When the tank is full, they'll finally be doing what they want to be doing with their time. Like the bucket, the tax code can be your friend or your foe. Some people assume the tax code, like the holey bucket, is all they will ever have to work with, while others figure out that the bucket and the tax code can be patched or fixed. Some adjust and modify, while most just drone on back and forth never really getting much done, accepting all the while that the deck is stacked against them.

There are essentially two income-taxing methods in the United States: one for the W-2 wage earner and the other for the self-employed. The W-2 wage earner carries the bucket with the holes (their income drains out to the IRS), but the self-employed individual has been gifted by the IRS a bucket that has been "patched," as it relates to our tax liabilities. This chapter will show you how to bring multiple tax minimization concepts and strategies to your tax planner that can be set up and administered under the guidance of your CPA or tax professional. As you will soon see, the self-employed enjoy many more tax deductions than W-2 wage earners. The self-employed are working with a different bucket! *For right now, never mind that you may be a W-2 wage earner.* I am not going to suggest you go out and quit your job. You can, however, keep your current job and begin a home-based business on the side that will do more for your wealth-creation dreams than perhaps any other financial strategy you might contemplate.

At some point in our lives, we all must realize that the largest expense our families will ever face is not our homes, educations, cars, food, or utilities. Our largest lifetime expense will be taxes. Yes, our taxes! Taxes will consume 40 to 65 percent of what most Americans earn, depending on their incomes. Most people are fuzzy about how much they are taxed and have no idea that with all the income, sales, property, death, investment, capital gains, state, federal, and miscellaneous taxes (like hotel taxes and license and registration taxes), they are often paying more than 50 percent of their incomes to the government. Of course, the government wisely invests in our futures so we do not have to worry about our own financial well being, right? Wrong!

We forget that, when we fill our gas tanks, fifty cents of the price of each gallon of gas is going to the government. Many people think only of their "take home" pay and don't think of the amount of money they actually earned as belonging to them. Moreover, many Americans never get around to estate-tax planning and disregard the fact that their taxable estate could be taxed by up to 45 percent. When you add it all up, we spend about one-half our calendar year working for the government.

> *The taxpayer: that's someone who works for the federal government, but doesn't have to take a civil service examination.*
>
> ~ President Ronald Reagan

I believe in paying taxes. I want a strong military and good roads and schools. I understand that police officers and firefighters need to get paid, and I see great value in many of the functions and benefits that our government provides. But I only want to pay my share, and I understand that my share should include a portion for those who are unable to contribute to our system. But I also figure I am more comfortable with 20 to 25 percent rather than 40 to 65 percent.)

So how do we calculate that? Our tax code is a complicated, convoluted, and confusing series of loops and measures that has been constructed, amended, protracted, and tweaked—perhaps more than any other document in the history of civilization.

This [preparing my tax return] is too difficult for a mathematician. It takes a philosopher.

~ Albert Einstein

Take a look at these statistics from the Heritage Foundation:

- Estimated time Americans will spend preparing their taxes this year: 6.4 billion hours
- Estimated amount Americans will spend on tax preparation: $265 billion
- Portion of Americans who will hire someone to prepare their taxes: 60 percent
- Increase in IRS rules and regulations over the last decade: 60.9 percent
- Number of new pages added to the Form 1040 instruction booklet in the last decade: 58

Ohio Congressman Rob Portman said, "The income tax code and its associated regulations contain almost 5.6 million words—seven times as many words as the Bible. Taxpayers now spend about 5.4 billion hours a year trying to comply with 2,500 pages of tax laws."

So what do we do? Most Americans assume that it is all too confusing and push the responsibility over to their tax professionals and CPAs. Here is the problem with that approach: you cannot pay a tax professional or CPA a couple of hundred dollars per year to prepare your tax return (essentially to record history) and expect that person to become your personal tax advocate and strategist. That's not their job! I have had clients tell me that their CPA takes care of their taxes. I think, *Really? Does Dr. Phil take care of your marriage? Does Kroger's take care of your nutritional needs? Does Joel Osteen take care of your faith?* Of course not. You have to be in the game in all of these important matters *yourself.* Your CPA or tax planner can implement your tax strategies, but you must bring the strategies and ideas to your tax professional in a tax-planning meeting that you initiate every six months. When was the last time your tax man called you and said, "Hey, I want you to come on over for about an hour. I have been sifting through your old 1040 returns along with some recent tax code changes, and I have some ideas and strategies that might save you and your family thousands of dollars in unnecessary taxes." You don't get that call, do you?

Think of your tax professional as a basketball referee. If you commit a foul, the ref can come over and tell you what you did wrong, but you don't expect him to call your next play. They are not getting paid for that. You and I must take the bull by the horns with self-education, tax planning, and choosing the right tax attorney or strategic tax planner. *Resolve to meet with your tax planner two times per year.* When you meet, bring notes, ideas, and articles that you have collected, including the strategies found in this chapter. You will soon find out if you have been working with a staunch paper pusher who only remembers the past or if you have a bright, innovative, and progressive tax planner who wants to help you avoid overpaying your taxes. If your tax man needs replacing, then throw him out! Call three friends whom you respect and who are more successful than you. Ask them whom they use. Tell them what you are looking for, and hope that two or more recommend the same person. Go in prepared, and let your tax planner know that you are working toward more effective tax planning and increasing your own fiscal literacy.

Most Americans are overpaying thousands of dollars per year that could be growing and compounding for their futures. Consider that if you overpay your taxes by $3,000 every year, you could be volunteering or forfeiting close to one million dollars—giving to the federal government money that would otherwise belong to your family. ($3,000 compounded over forty years at 8 percent is $904,516.) I believe that many middle class families are overpaying closer to $6,000 every year, giving away close to 2 million dollars over their working lives. Enough already!

Eight Relevant Tax Strategies You Can Use Now

1. Start a Home-Based Business

Owning a business is the best tax shelter in America today. This is because business owners have many more deductions than employees. A former IRS tax attorney once said, "You would have to be brain-dead not to own a home-based business." That got my attention. You don't need to quit your job to launch a small business; you only need an idea. Your home-based business and structure will allow you to reposition many of your existing and new expenses into legal and legitimate itemized business expenses, potentially lowering both your marginal and your effective tax rate.

Sample Federal Tax Rate Schedule

Tax Rate	Single Filers	Married Filing Jointly
10 %	up to $8,025	up to $16,050
15 %	$8,026–$32,550	$16,051–$65,100
25 %	$32,551–$78,850	$65,101–$131,450
28 %	$78,851–$164,550	$131,451–$200,300
33 %	$164,551–$357,700	$200,301–357,700
35 %	$357,701 or more	$357,701 or more

Note: Lowering your adjusted gross income (AGI), sometimes by just a small amount, may move you into a lower marginal tax bracket.

Let's look at an example. Rita Tutorsmore has a college degree and excelled in math and science in school. Years ago she and her husband decided that she would stay home and raise their children and her husband would be the primary breadwinner. In talking with other mothers in the neighborhood, Rita found that several of their kids needed tutoring and many of the moms were looking for someone in their community to help for just a few hours a week. Rita began tutoring students in her home, and after meeting with her CPA, determined that she could form a business and turn many of her expenses into legitimate business expenses. Rita formed a company, began taking a home office deduction, and set up a medical expense reimbursement plan that employs her spouse. Rita pays her spouse only in benefits. Now all of the family's nonreimbursed medical expenses, including insurance premiums, doctor office co-pays, deductibles, and noncovered costs become expensed to the family under the plan. With the home office deduction a portion of the bills for electricity, the security system, the phone, pool service, cable TV, yard maintenance, the mortgage, and property taxes are all expensed to Rita's company.

Now much of Rita's travel, entertainment, and automobile expenses are deductions because Rita drives to meet families who are considering her services. Often she lunches with mothers who are potential clients, and Rita usually manages to conduct some business when she travels, making a portion of her family vacations deductible. As a business owner, Rita is permitted to save and invest more aggressively in tax-deferred investment accounts reserved only for business owners (at the time of writing, an annual SEP Plan contribution of $46,000 is allowed). As a result of Rita's tax planning, she and her family now have ten thousand dollars in total expenses, which moves the family from the 28-percent tax bracket to the 25-percent bracket. Rita and her family estimate that the new home business saves the family about five thousand dollars in income taxes simply by optimizing the rules of the IRS code. If Rita and her family invest in real estate and paper assets averaging 9 percent return over thirty years, she and her husband calculate that this strategy alone will be worth approximately 2 million dollars over their working careers. Rita initially wonders why everyone does not optimize legal tax strategies, but then she remembers that these concepts were only revealed to her once she invested a few hours in reading a tax strategies book while she was on vacation while others around her were reading romance novels, John Grisham books, and *People* magazine.

Your CPA or tax attorney can determine with you if your business should be a C corporation, S corporation, LLC, LLP, or sole proprietorship. Some of the determining factors will be the nature of the business, the amount of revenue anticipated, and whether or not your business will contain real estate. Your tax professional can also provide you with the IRS-approved framework and rules to administer your medical expense reimbursement plan, and your deductions for your home office, automobile, meals, entertainment, travel, and other expenses.

A self-started home-based business could consist of consulting, tutoring, distributing, marketing, bookkeeping, writing, training, or a variety of other services. You can come up with your own concept, or if you prefer working with a structure that is already in place, you may wish to consider companies such as Arbonne, Mary Kay, Stream Energy, Juice Plus+, Pre-Paid Legal Service, World Financial Group, and Southern Home Living. A home-based business is easier than most people think, and with a good tax professional by your side, the benefits can be astonishing and life-changing.

2. Invest in Real Estate

There are many different types of investment real estate—rental houses, apartments, vacant land, commercial buildings, industrial property, shopping centers, warehouses, and more—and they all offer big tax incentives for investors who understand these benefits.

The IRS allows investors to depreciate their investment properties, and this powerful strategy can be a critical tool in working toward your wealth goals. *Depreciation is the best real estate tax deduction of all.* Depreciation is a "loss" that accounts for estimated wear, tear, and obsolescence. (Residential income property is depreciated over 27.5 years on a straight-line basis. Commercial property is depreciated over 39 years, also on a straight-line basis.) Land value is not depreciable. Condominiums do not have a land element, so 100 percent of the purchase price can be depreciated. Almost all investment properties go up in value each year, but on your tax returns their values go down. I like that!

You may wish to go back and reread the chapter on real estate investing for more clarity on depreciation.

3. Setup a Medical Expense Reimbursement Account

Did you know that your home-based business can hire your spouse and pay him or her only in benefits? No salary is required under IRS guidelines. Benefits can be provided through a medical expense reimbursement plan. The plan that is adopted by your home-based business can reimburse your spouse for medical expenses that are not covered under any other plan. The benefits are for an individual (in this case, your spouse), their children, and you.

Under the plan (IRS Section 105) your spouse can be reimbursed for office co-pays, deductibles, and uncovered costs. This can include your child's braces, your eyeglasses, LASIK corrective eye surgery, and much more.

Tell your CPA to see IRS Publication 502. Below is a list of allowable deductions taken from IRS Publication 502.

- Acupuncture
- Abdominal supports
- Air conditioners*
- Alcohol treatment
- Artificial limbs/teeth
- Automobile equipment to assist the physically disabled
- Back supports
- Bereavement and grief counseling
- Birth control pills
- Bone marrow transplants
- Braille books and magazines
- Co-pays for prescription drugs, including birth control pills and insulin
- Cosmetic surgery or procedure for a deformity from congenital abnormality, an accident or trauma, or a disfiguring disease

- Crutches
- Deductibles (except for HDHP with HSA) and co-pays for health care and dental expenses
- Dental care, including orthodontia and implant expenses (unless it is for cosmetic purposes)
- Detoxification or drug abuse center care
- Diagnostic tests
- Diathermy
- Doctor's fees
- Doctor's office visits
- Drug addiction treatment
- Eyeglasses and fees for eye exams
- Guides or guide dogs for visually or hearing impaired
- Hearing aid exams, hearing aids, and supplies
- Hospital services
- Infertility treatment
- Insulin, syringes, test strips and bits

- In vitro fertilization
- Lab fees
- Lamaze classes
- Learning disability tuition*
- Massage therapy*
- Medical alert bracelet
- Medically necessary mattresses and boards*
- Mental health or substance abuse expenses
- Note taker for hearing-impaired child in school
- Nursing services
- Optometrist fees
- Organ donation expenses
- Organ transplants
- Orthodontia (see Dental Care, above)
- Orthopedic shoes/inserts*
- Over-the-counter (OTC) drugs such as antacids, allergy medicine, and pain relievers

- Physical therapy
- Physician examination
- Prescription drugs
- Psychiatrist/psychologist fees
- Psychoanalysis (unless required of students in psychoanalytic training institutions)
- Periodontal fees
- Radial keratotomy, RPK, or LASIK eye surgery
- Radiation treatments
- Remedial reading*
- Rental of medical equipment
- Respirators
- Routine physical exams
- Sales tax and shipping and handling fees associated with an eligible expense
- Smoking cessation programs and prescription drugs
- Specialized equipment for disabled persons

- Speech therapy
- Sterilization surgery*
- Surgery Therapy for mental/nervous disorders
- Travel allowance/lodging for out-of-town care
- Vaccinations
- Weight loss programs or medications*
- Well-baby and well-child care
- Wheelchairs
- Wigs for hair loss due to any disease*
- X-rays

*Expenses must be accompanied by a physician's certification specifying the disorder, the treatment needed, and how the treatment will alleviate the condition.

4. Deduct Entertainment, Meals, and Vacations

The IRS allows you to deduct the cost of the meals with five pieces of information: cost, date, location (these three are all on your receipt), purpose of your discussion, and your relationship to your guest. You do not even need a receipt for expenses under seventy-five dollars! The IRS rule reads that you can deduct the cost for meals with a bona fide business purpose, which would include meetings with clients, prospects, business colleagues, and referral sources. In my home-based education business almost every person I come into contact with fits one of these IRS-approved categories.

You can forget about trying to write these costs off under W-2 wages as nonreimbursed business expenses. The IRS has this method so watered down it will not be worth the administrative cost to keep track of these expenses. The desired outcome for you is to have your home-based business approved and legitimate expenses wash out your W-2 income dollar for dollar.

With respect to travel, according to the IRS you are on business travel when you are traveling from home for a specific business purpose, either overnight or for a period of time sufficient to require sleep. By keeping close and careful records of your travel and by combining legitimate business activities you can legally expense much of your travel costs to the IRS.

When I travel I am usually doing one of the following things:

- attending a seminar;
- visiting referral sources for my business;

or

- care-taking for my out-of-town rental property (The IRS says that necessary travel to take care of my rental property is tax-deductible. My family owns a ski condo in the mountains that we stay in sometimes and also rent out others; so when I am there I make sure to spend—and document—time checking on comparable rental rates, the property condition, and the fee structure of the management company. These are all legitimate business activities and meet the IRS rcquirements for legitimate business travel).

Insist that your Tax Planner is providing you the IRS-compliant structure and framework for deductions in this area. You will be wise to have your CPA sign off on your return, as no one wants to creep into gray areas and cheating on your taxes is not an option.

5. Take a Home Office Deduction

I'll bet someone has told you that a home office deduction is a red flag for an IRS audit, right? *Not so!* This has not been the case for years; and in many cases the IRS does not even know that you are taking the deduction because of the absence of any required form. The home office deduction is likely the most misunderstood deduction in our entire tax code.

The IRS says you can take the home office deduction if you use it exclusively and regularly and if you have no other fixed location where you conduct substantial administrative or management activities of your trade or business. Let your CPA guide you through the rest; but do not just accept from your CPA that this is a red flag, and do not be afraid to take this legitimate IRS-approved deduction if you have a legitimate home based business. Create and maintain good records.

6. Optimize Your Car

One real estate agent I know drives a Toyota Prius, and another agent I know drives a four-wheel-drive Ford Excursion. The IRS gives both the option to either deduct actual expenses when the vehicles are used for business or to deduct 50.5 cents per mile. I am fairly sure the agent with the Excursion has much higher car payments and pays much higher fuel, insurance, maintenance, and repair costs, but that is not a concern for the IRS. The deduction method choice is the same for all drivers and for all automobiles. Most people find that their accountant does not care either and will usually choose the default path of deduction by the mile. This is the wrong answer for the guy with the Excursion, Lexus, or SUV! For many people some simple math will reveal that they would be better served by selecting the actual expense method and tracking their expenses and mileage with good accounting and a diary.

The IRS wants your travel costs to be logged "at or near the time" when you incur the expense. Good records and accounting insure that you will never have to fear an audit or inquiry of any sort from the IRS. I make all of this my bookkeeper's responsibility and report my records to her daily. Most would be wise to do the same. My bookkeeper works for me part-time and has a CPA to work with. The CPA is under the direction of my tax attorney. Once they have direction from me, they construct the accounting methods and structure for accurately documenting these expenses. You would be wise to set up a similar system. I have met people who try to save a few hundred dollars by compiling all of the records themselves, but I always feel better knowing the records are produced by my professional associates rather than by me.

7. Meet with a Tax and Estate Attorney

Perhaps one of the best investments of your time and money will be to meet with a good tax and estate Attorney. Take to the meeting two years of filed tax returns, a personal financial statement, your will, and an agenda of what you wish to speak about. If you have an idea as to what kind of home business you want to start, your attorney will be able to advise you on the most suitable legal entity type and structure. Your attorney will let you know if you have or are headed toward potential estate planning problems and can provide appropriate solutions. Your will and medical directives should also be reviewed at this meeting.

The visit could be free, but if there is a fee, most attorneys will charge around two hundred to three hundred dollars. You will soon realize the wide scope of options and strategies that are available to you. *Don't skimp on this!* One endeavor of this book is to enlighten you as to some of the options that are available to all Americans. A good tax and estate Attorney can ensure that your business activities, estate planning, and tax strategies all sit on a firm and suitable foundation.

If you have an estate valued at over two

million dollars (including the death benefit if your life insurance pays off) you could be subject to an estate tax of 45 percent—that's nine hundred thousand dollars. While one spouse can die and pass assets to the other spouse with no tax on any limit, when the living spouse dies, the estate gets hammered. A good tax attorney will provide a simple solution to this potential tax problem. I will discuss this further in the final chapter of this book. *Make sure to talk to your tax attorney about estate taxes!*

8. Work with an Advisory Team that Understands Buckets

The Four Buckets

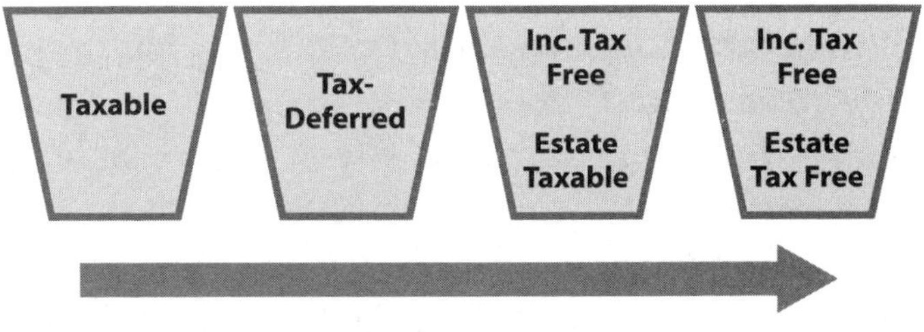

Any income or assets we have will fall into one of the four buckets:

1. Bucket 1 is Taxable. This would be your W2 paystub or your 1099.

2. Bucket 2 is Tax Deferred. This would be any QP (Qualified Plan) such as IRA, 401(k), 457 Plan, 403(b), SEP, or any other tax deferred plan, as well as some NQ (non-qualified) annuities.

3. Bucket 3 is Tax Free. This would be muni bonds, life insurance and ROTH IRAs. *These are the only 3 things that are income tax free!*

4. Bucket 4 is Income Tax Free and Estate Tax Free. This would include certain trusts that would be formed in estate planning. Please see the final chapter of this book for more details on this bucket.

The more income and assets that you have, the more important it becomes to learn how to shift and move income and assets from left to right in these buckets.

As you will see in the chart listed below. Tax deferred is more attractive than taxed as earned and tax free is better than tax deferred.

Taxable vs. Tax Advantage

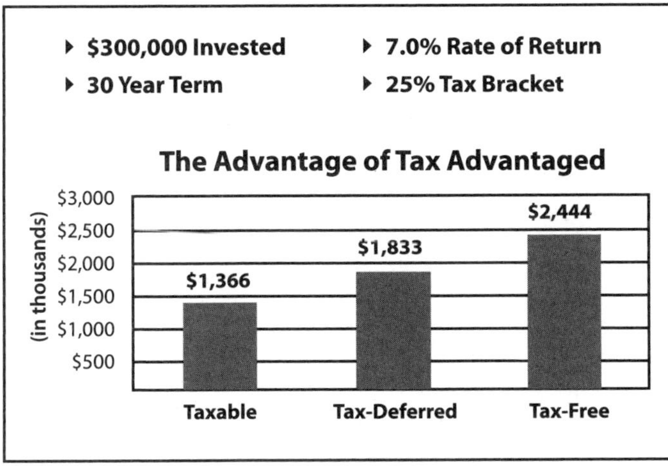

Show this chart to your advisory team and ask them if they understand this concept and if the planning they are providing for you can help you shift income and assets from left to right. If you get a blank stare, MOVE ON.

Fiscal Literacy Points

- Taxes are your biggest lifetime expense.
- Most Americans overpay taxes due to a lack of fiscal literacy.
- Begin a home-based business and take advantage of the tax benefits.

- Set up a medical expense reimbursement plan.
- Don't fear the home office deduction.
- Meet with a tax attorney.
- Shift income and assets from left to right in the four buckets

Please note that the author and his affiliates do not advise on any personal income tax requirements or issues, and the author is not a licensed tax advisor. Any information presented in this publication or the associated Web site is for general information only and does not represent personal tax advice of any kind either expressed or implied. You are encouraged to seek professional tax advice for all personal tax questions and assistance. IRS tax guidelines change regularly.

Chapter Six

Optimize Your Retirement Account and Investments

Why do some win at investing and others lose playing the same game? The answer is once again fiscal literacy. Remember the masses are playing checkers while the wealthy are playing chess. So is true with our investments. In our practice we help clients determine what percentage of their money should be kept safe, and how much do we want to have at risk.

For the amount of money that we want to have safe we use tools like investment grade bonds, TIPS (Treasury Inflation Protected Securities) UIT's, T- Bills, Notes and Bonds, STRIPS and certain types of principal protected annuities.

The common problem we see when clients lose big with their investments is that they have chosen on purpose or by default, or even by taking bad advice, to take on too much risk. Let me say that another way. Most investors take on far too much unnecessary risk.

Some of our money must always be SAFE, less we chose the road-kill path of the masses who have all but given up on the stock market. The safe percentage will be determined by your risk tolerance and other factors.

While this chapter will cover multiple ways to invest like the wealthy please do not mistake the strategies for lack of long term faith in equities. We believe in the stock market at my firm, we just want our cake and to eat it to. I believe in my Chevy Truck to take me down the road and to where I want to go, but I don't drive too fast, I buckle up, and I drive a truck with airbags. Same with stocks; we want the growth opportunity, but we don't just jump off a cliff with naked long stock positions or a traditional "balanced" portfolio. As we learned in the market meltdown in 2008; in a "balanced portolio" everything can go down at the same time.

For money that is in stocks I recommend that you work with advisors that use strategies like covered calls, negatively correlated asset portfolios, structured equity investments, absolute return portfolios, and ETF Indexing. Work with someone who actively manages your positions with stop loss orders and buy limits. Don't settle for a "set it and forget it" type of mutual fund advisor. You can do better!

Buy mutual funds and diversify

Thanks to the voice of Wall Street, this is the mantra of the masses. Without question, the single most common message that can be heard across America today regarding investing is to buy mutual funds and diversify. It sounds logical, right? Spread your money across large segments of industry and own many different companies inside a liquid vehicle. In my 401(k), I can own ten different kinds of funds with each fund owning more than fifty companies. With one click of the mouse my money can be spread all over the free world and participate in over five hundred different companies, sectors, and investments ranging from real estate REITs and bond funds to small-, medium-, and large-cap stocks, foreign markets, and so on. Sounds safe and easy, right? Moreover, every time I tune in to listen to a personal finance guru on the radio or pick up the latest magazine on managing my investments, the common message resounds loud and clear: *buy mutual funds and diversify.* As the statistics deomstrate, most Americans have bought into this ideal.

Some Americans, however, avoid the default path of the masses and invest differently. They invest like the wealthy. Fiscal literacy makes all the difference here. Unlike the denizens of Middle America, the wealthy continued to create wealth even when the market crashed at the end of the 1990s. The average American lost almost 40 percent of his or her retirement savings between the years 2000 and 2002. During this time mutual fund companies' messages became "We are not losing as much money as our competitors."

On January 15, 2000, the Dow was at 11,792. In late 2008, almost nine years later, the Dow sat at just over 8,200. Sadly, over this period most Americans lost approximately 66 percent of their nest eggs. *How's that?*, you ask. Well, think about it: Let's say I lost 30 percent of my money to the market and I lost an additional 4 percent per year to inflation over nine years: 36 percent plus 30 percent equals a 66-percent loss. In addition to my losses, I incurred a lost opportunity cost. If I had been earning only 6 percent on my money, the overall losses amount to 100 percent. There is a lost opportunity cost that broker and mutual fund sellers fail to acknowledge when we are losing time and losing money.

Complete this sentence for me: Time is _______. When we lose money in the markets, we are also losing time and accumulating huge losses with opportunity cost.

Now wait just a cotton-picking minute! Am I telling you that the greatest minds on Wall

Street—you know, Merrill Lynch (which lost almost everything and was bought for pennies on the dollar by Bank of America); Fannie Mae and Freddie Mac; Bear Stearns, Goldman Sachs, Lehman Brothers, and WaMu; and company after company that went down in flames during one of our many financial crises over the past one hundred years–have been pushing a financial formula that might leave you and me broke in our retirement years? *That's exactly what I'm telling you.*

And am I also telling you that the wealthy follow a different path? That they structure their investments in ways that eliminate losses, give simple compounding returns, and offer multiple market participation methods? *Yes, I am!*

And here is a surprise for you: it's not just the wealthy anymore. More and more Americans are increasing their fiscal literacy today because they have to. More Americans are rejecting the default path of the masses and choosing financial concepts once reserved for the wealthiest people. This chapter will show you how to join their ranks regardless of your current net worth or status.

But, you may be thinking, *my broker says that the accounts always come back from losses.* Yes, historically, that is a true statement. But if you have an account with $100,000 that goes down 50 percent one year and then up 50 percent the next, will you be coming out even? Let's see.

Year 1: $100,000 after a 50-percent loss equals $50,000.

Year 2: $50,000 after a 50-percent gain equals $75,000.

My money would have to go up 100 percent in year 2 to make up for a 50-percent loss in year 1. This is why a market that averaged 10.2 percent over eighty years earned investors only 4 to 6 percent. That is nuts! To me, earning 4 to 6 percent when we are asked to risk it all is unreasonable, especially when there are far better options available. In the example above, after a down-50-percent year and an up-50-percent year, I would still be negative 25 percent, not including the losses on what my money could have earned. If I had earned 6 percent over the two-year period, I would have been able to add another 12 percent to my earnings; adding this 12-percent lost opportunity cost to my negative 25 percent puts me at a loss of 37 percent.

I will tell you who wins in this picture, and it is not me; it is the broker who was getting paid every year regardless of whether I won or lost. They call it "assets under management," and there are great rewards, compensation, accolades, and trips for salespeople who hold the most assets under management. These are usually the very best and charismatic salespeople who can convince the public that the buy-and-hold strategy—"The market always comes back, right?"—will work for their clients. They never inform their clients of the staggering damage that market losses bring to their nest eggs because they do not want to lose the assets under management.

I have a challenge for you. Reflect on your own holdings and ask yourself if this strategy has worked for you. I think we both know the answer. Now look at the following example, and consider that, while liquidity is important, our primary focus in investing is for income in retirement. A qualified advisor can help you determine what a suitable asset mix would encompass. Most families are too heavily weighted in asset classes that represent too much risk. Consider what can be accomplished in guaranteeing income in retirement with an indexed annuity. A indexed annuity with an income rider can give guaranteed returns to the income value of the account and allow the principal to participate in market returns. One might realize about 60 percent of the stock market gains to the accumulation value of the account *and* never lose any money when the stock market goes down. This is how an FIA account works with an income rider.

S&P 500 Actual Returns
LAST TEN YEARS
(2008 Estimate)
(S&P is a trademark of McGraw-Hill)

or

Guaranteed Fixed Account
7.2-PERCENT INCOME VALUE
FIA Structured Hybrid

Our investor must decide how to invest $100,000.

Wall Street			Protected Account		
Year	**Change**	**Amount**	**Year**	**Change**	**Amount**
1999	+19.51%	$119,510	1999	+7.2%	$107,200
2000	-10.14%	$107,391	2000	+7.2%	$114,918
2001	-13.04%	$93,387	2001	+7.2%	$123,192
2002	-23.37%	$71,562	2002	+7.2%	$132,061
2003	+26.39%	$90,449	2003	+7.2%	$141,569
2004	+9.00%	$98,589	2004	+7.2%	$151761
2005	+3.01%	$101,645	2005	+7.2%	$162,687
2006	+12.8%	$114,655	2006	+7.2%	$174,400
2007	+3.81%	$119,023	2007	+7.2%	$186,956
2008	-35.00%	$77,364	2008	+7.2%	$200,423

**2008 Results are estimates at this time.*

END RESULT

Wall Street **$77,364**	**Protected Account** **$200,416**
Down 23% Over Ten Years	Average Rate Of Return
Return average: -2.3 percent per year	Return average: 7.2 percent (Income Value)
Effective average loss: 3.8 percent	Almost 3 times the performance No losses, no fees
(includes management cost of 1.5 percent)	
Client risks everything!	Principal Protected Accounts
Income at 6% per year = $4,700 year	**Income at 6% per year = $12,000 year**

Investment Return vs. Investor Return

When a broker shows clients a chart on the wall with the long-term Dow *investment* return averaging over 10 percent over the past eighty years what they fail to tell them is that the average *investor* return is 4 to 6 percent. During a 20 year period beginning in the mid 80's, the stock market has averaged a 12-percent annual return. But according to a study by Dalbar Financial, individual mutual fund investors earned only about 4 percent. A survey by Vanguard finds participants in its 401(k) plans earn only about one-half the average—6 percent a year. It is unpleasant to contemplate, but practically all individual investors are below average. (Source: Slate.com)

The Stock Market Myth and Why Investors Must Change Their Way of Thinking About the Stock Market

When you ask most people why they have significant exposure to the stock market they will usually say that they have been shown data that that shows that the stock market is where they will earn the greatest return on their money over time, and you know what; there is a kernel of truth to that suggestion. If you can time the market just right or if you have enough time on your hands the stock market can yield robust returns, and even robust decades.

As you have now found by reading this far in Live Smart-Retire Rich there is often more to the story and more information that you need to know before you go down the default path that the typical Financial Advisor will prescribe to you.

Let's look a little closer at the data going back to 1900 (Source Dow Jones website at www.djindexes.com.)

Decade	Return	Return +3% Dividend
1900 – 1909	+4.19%	+7.19%
1910 – 1919	+0.80%	+3.80%
1920 – 1929	+8.77%	+11.77%
1930 – 1939	-4.92%	-1.92%
1940 – 1949	+2.95%	+5.95%
1950 – 1959	+12.98%	+15.98%
1960 – 1969	+1.65%	+4.65%
1970 – 1979	+0.47%	+3.47%
1980 – 1989	+12.62%	+15.62%
1990 – 1999	+15.37%	+18.37%
2000 – 2008	-2.96%	+0.04%
Average Return	**+4.72%**	**+7.72%**

Six of the past eleven decades the the stock market did not even beat 6% for the decade !! – But when it does it can be really good, take the 80's or the 90's for example. Now if you're in your 20's to 40's and you have 30 years on your side the stock market can be a decent bet for you over the long haul, but what if you are in your 60's or 70's ? Do you really want significant exposure to a crap shoot that can be so fickle? Many Financial Advisors in their quest for assets under management ignore data that they know exists and place their own personal interests above their clients, making recommendations that will work only for their clients in a "best case" scenario. This is pathetic and unconscionable to me.

Once we start looking at all the data by decades, the data becomes very clear. The data doesn't support an average return worth betting the farm on, and that is a message that big brokerage firms would prefer not to get out as this would really throw a monkey wrench in their "assets under management" mantra.

Many Financial Advisors tell their clients that it is reasonable to expect a 10% average return because "that's what the market averages over time." The problem is that 10 years is clearly not enough time to have any reasonable expectation of hitting that average. In fact, 20 years is also not long enough. As a result, millions of Americans may fall well short in their entire retirement years, never reaching their investment expectations because of either bad advice or an underperforming decade with just a few negative years. It only takes one or two down years to kill the return of an entire decade.

Fortunately, other options exist, including fixed and hybrid investments, to assist investors in protecting against those very downturns that can kill you. Since you can anticipate these types of downturns every two out of three decades, you would be wise to consider other options to immunize your retirement portfolio against significant risk.

You and I are investors not investments. Investor returns are much lower than investment returns because you and I are people. People have emotions. We get excited and buy when the market is high, and we get fearful and sell when the market is tanking. This is human nature, and it is the largest reason investor returns are so low. The secondary consideration is the fees that the brokers and mutual fund sellers charge. They charge their fees, commissions, loads, expenses, 12b-1 fees, and operating costs regardless of whether you win or lose.

I want you to say out loud right now that these returns are unacceptable given the risk you must take. If we are going to risk losing our life savings for a documented investor return average of 4 to 6 percent, then God help us—and shame on us as Americans for not increasing our fiscal literacy and ensuring our future with financial strategies that offer better returns, less risk, and more tax advantages.

I once hired a guy to work on my computer; but his "help" only made the problem worse, and he could not provide a solution to my computer's failure. The technician did not have the gall or justification to give me a bill, but Wall Street does! On average, brokers will bill you 1.5 to 2% percent on your account balance—win or lose. If you lose 15 percent, it really amounts to 16.5 percent once their fees are tacked on. Disgusting!

What does the stock market do? It goes up. It goes down. It goes up. It goes down. Americans jump on the bandwagon when the market is hot; and they usually panic and sell for a loss when it is low. If you can keep a straight face and tell me that you can win at this gambit, then I say you are smarter than I am. No one wins at gambling for very long and neither will you. Your broker will be the winner in the final analysis.

This is how money works for the masses, because most people are fooled by the Wall Street establishment whose primary interest is assets under management. When the chips are down, what do they say? "Hang in there! It takes discipline. The market will go back up." Give me a break! Some say they're called brokers because the longer you stay with them, the broker you are!

Think you're a stock picker? Which one of the following stocks would you have purchased back in 2003?

Wal-Mart	**Kmart**
• One of largest companies in the world	• Just emerging from bankruptcy
• Consistent earner	• Big marketing tie to Martha Stewart
• Pays dividends	• No anticipated dividends
Stock Price July 11, 2003	
$56.08	$24.20
Stock Price July 11, 2004	
$51.76	$76.80

Which one would you have chosen? Most people would have opted for Wal-Mart and lost money instead of buying Kmart and earning significant gains.

How We Lose Money In Sideways Stock Market

(Phantom Shrinkage)

$100,000 IN ONE YEAR

Account value opens January 1 at $100,000 and closes December 31 at $86,960
The account had equal gains and losses, but the value of the account still shrinks.

Month	Return	Amount
Begin		**$ 100,000**
January	- 15%	$ 85,000
February	+ 15%	$ 97,750
March	- 20%	$ 78,200
April	+ 20%	$ 93,840
May	- 10%	$ 84,456
June	+ 10%	$ 92,901
July	- 15%	$ 92,901
August	+ 15%	$ 90,811
September	- 20%	$ 72,649
October	+ 20%	$ 87,178
November	- 5%	$ 82,819
December	+ 5%	**$ 86,960**

Account Value December 31, net of fees:
Approximately $86,000

This one-year example of a sideways market illustrates how money is lost in normal market fluctuations. Notice that the market is even for the year, but our money has lost almost 13 percent because as the market recovers, we are starting with a lower account value. Now consider that on top of that we likely paid a 1.5-percent management fee. *The combined losses amount to over 14 percent!*

Most Americans have no idea why their investment accounts are consistent underachievers. All the while they are told by Wall Street to hang in there and that things will get better. Things will get better, all right. They will get better when you fire the the advisor whose flawed logic recommends that you gamble with the security of your retirement.

The wealthy figured out the fallacy of this flawed amateur trap long ago. They have enough money to tell their investment firms to build complex monetization strategies with options, puts, and calls around leveraged stock positions. With ten million dollars in a blue chip firm you have access to an entire team of financial architects who will ensure that you will never lose your money to stock market losses and that you will average the highest possible investor returns. The wealthy have their cake, and when they eat it, it's served on a silver platter by a waiter in pinstripes.

Complete this sentence for me, will you? The rich get _______. Thank you! Remember Warren Buffet's first rule of investing: "Never, ever lose your money."

One of my dearest friends, whose mother is in her late sixties, went in to her broker and complained that her account had not grown and in fact had lost a great deal of money over the past several years. The broker had the temerity to brag that the funds at his firm had not lost as much as his peers' funds, and he insisted that the chart on his wall proved that the long-term future of the equities market could assure her that one day her account would be back to a positive status.

If I had been there, I might have smacked him!

On its best day, this logic only works for those with long horizons, those in their twenties and thirties. Never mind that even these young people *still* could do much better in a the nontraditional environment of structured products and protected accounts that many of the investment firms and insurance companies are offering today. agree that we need some stock market exposure as a hedge against inflation, but too many people take on too much risk and later wonder what went wrong. Poor planning and or poor advice are usually the answer.

Don't forget that the Rule of 100 says to start with the number 100 and subtract your age. The number left over is the percentage that you should have at risk in the market. A 70 year old should not have more than about 30% of his assets at risk. While this rule is not hard and fast for all investors it serves as a good starting point in determining how much money to protect and how much is going to be at risk. I define at risk as any investment that could lose 20% or more in one year !

Safety in Bonds?

Today, many are concerned about the volatility of the stock market and the decline of their mutual funds, so bonds are often looked at to provide a higher level of security, however bonds have their own risks which include risk of default, call, loss of principal, credit rating, and interest rate fluctuations. Bonds have their appropriate time, proportion and place. In over simplified terms we want to buy more bonds when interest rates are high and fewer bonds when interest rates are low. Right now as I write this the Fed Funds rate is zero. We do not anticipate rates going lower. To understand bonds better think of a see-saw in a neighborhood playground. When one kid goes up the other goes where ? Down, right ? - The same is true with bond values and interest rate.

If interest rates are going up. the value of bonds are headed down. When interest rates are headed down, the value and yield of our bonds grow. Do you see why we favor bonds when interest rates are at their higher levels and are more likely to be headed downward ? Again, lots to know here and to be considered in purchasing bonds. Make sure your Advisor understands how and when to use bonds in your portfolio and stay away from product sales people who are also sometimes called "financial advisor." You shouldn't think that you can always get out of the rain in bonds, as bond earnings struggle to maintain pace with inflation and cannot provide the growth needed to fund your retirement when you are fortunate enough to live longer than you had anticipated. I have a good friend whose father lost 90% of his portfolio in GM bonds that his advisor had assured him were safe. Most financial advisors tell their clients that their money is safe and conservatively invested in bonds. You may also recall that in late 2008 the FDIC had an emergency policy to cover money market funds for a period of time as most "investors" assumed that money markets were as safe as CDs. They are not!

> *If you thought the 2000–2002 crash was painful, think again! It barely made the list of the ten worst markets crashes in U.S. history.*
>
> ~ Dustin Woodard

It's all in the timing. In October of 2006, *Money* magazine published an article stating that, according to Ibbotson Associates, if I had retired in 1973 with one million dollars in a "balanced portfolio" of 60 percent stocks and 40 percent bonds and had withdrawn fifty thousand dollars every year to live on, my account balance would have hit zero in twenty years. The reason for this would have been that I had retired into a bear market and overall the markets experienced a slow, downward trend.

Conversely, if I had retired ten years later in 1983 (a bull-market period) with the same portfolio of stocks and bonds and the same annual withdrawals of fifty thousand dollars, twenty years later my account balance would be over five million dollars. Holy smokes! These statistics tell us all two things. First, market timing is everything; and second, we have no idea what the market timing is going to look like in each of our individual retirement pictures. What is the market timing going to be when you retire? *We don't know!* Are you going to be rich? Or are you going to run out of money before you run out of you and become a burden to your children? Most Americans are depending on a best-case scenario for their retirements in their 401(k) s and mutual funds thanks to the voice of the mutual fund establishment. I completely reject this level of wishful thinking, and I encourage you to join me and not leave your future and your retirement to a Wall Street casino mentality that could leave you shaking hands at Wal-Mart in your golden years. Wall Street cares about assets under management. That is it in a nutshell. They get paid every year regardless if you are winning or losing.

FIAs, hybrids, and safe money strategies such as structured investments are where many Americans are finding they can have their cakes and eat them, too. This goes for your IRA and any other money that you do not care to lose. While many Wall Street firms offer structured investments where their clients' money is guaranteed against loss, the entry point can be rather steep for some. Many of these vehicles require five hundred thousand dollars or more and have become extremely popular among affluent Americans as they have said no to Wall Street losses.

Middle America can effectively participate in a similar structure with a type of fixed annuity called an *equity-indexed annuity* (EIA). Indexed annuities protect their owners against market losses and offer much of the market upside when the market does well.

Let me say that again: Fixed indexed annuities let you sleep at night. You do not have to worry about losing your money, and they give you the market upside when the market does perform in your favor.

Indexed annuities have IRS-approved deferral of income and taxes as established in Section 72 of the IRS code. Fee-based financial planners have known for years that annuities can be one of the most valuable tools in helping clients avoid taxes on Social Security income. Fee-based financial planners regularly recommend EIAs as solutions as these financial planners are not primarily concerned with assets under management. Most annuities also have a feature that allows you to exchange your account value for an income stream at a future date. This feature, called annuitized, could be an important feature for some. I own indexed annuities because of their market security. At this time I have no plans to exchange my cash value for an income stream, but it is handy to know that that feature exists should I ever elect to do so. I should note, however, that I never *have* to trade my cash for income inside my contract, and most annuities never make any such requirement.

My indexed annuities have been far greater performers than the mutual funds inside my 401(k). I know there are many who are wishing for a repeat of the 1990s when cab drivers, monkeys with darts, and sixth-grade investment students were all accomplished stock pickers. I guess if that time comes around again I might not get some of the gains that the gamblers will, but I would bet the safety and security of my retirement plan—along with its eventual outcome and performance—against the Wall Street establishment money scheme any day.

Triple Compounding

Fixed EIA contracts allow for triple compound interest, which means that your initial investment or principle earns interest, your interest earns interest, and the dollars you would have paid in taxes earn interest.

Taxable vs. Tax Deferred

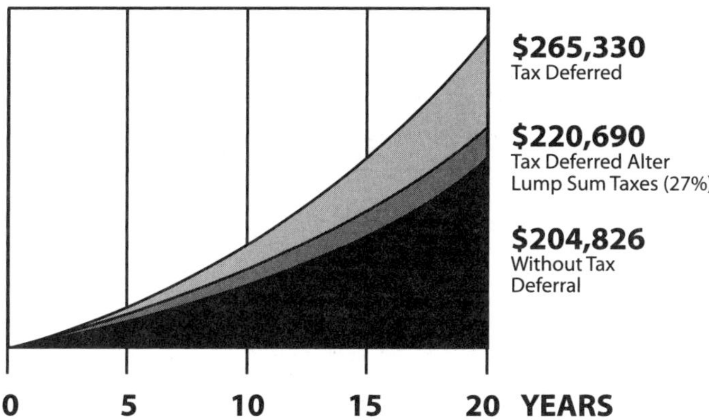

Note: Example assumes 5% annual interest rate and 27% tax bracket

Annuities and most insurance products took a bad rap in the 1980s and 1990s because they were not structured like the sophisticated instruments that they are today. In decades past they were poor performers with heavy fees, and their contracts were confusing even to the people who sold them. I believe that during this time the insurance companies earned the bad rap that they received; but today products are different and sit on a different chassis. Today's indexed annuities offer a cost-efficient method to compound your dollars in a safe account that will not lose when the market goes down. The annuity owner gives up about 40 percent of the market upside when the market does well, which most people would have to agree is a great exchange for the downside protection.

The table below shows how market protection against losses is a must if you plan to live smart and retire rich and if you plan to move up your financial freedom date.

The key to why index annuities perform so well is simple: they never show a loss. Richard Russell, founder and editor of *The Dow Theory Letter*, said, "He who loses least … wins!" With index annuities, we never lose. Index annuities without caps are excellent vehicles for your financial security. Enjoy the gain, and eliminate the pain.

S&P 500 vs. Annual Point-to-Point (2000-2005)

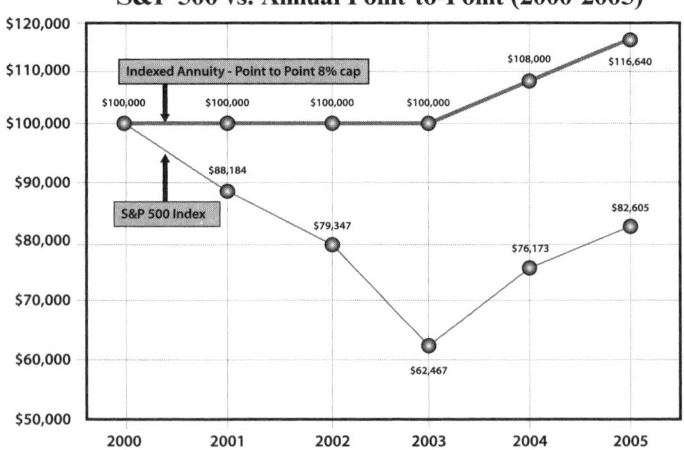

Now consider what the market has done through the end of 2008. I bet locking in your gains and avoiding market losses is looking better and better!

The mutual fund establishment regularly blasts annuities and other insurance products and accuses them of having excessive and bloated fees and costs, causing them to be poor performers. I would have to agree that the dated products of the 1980s did deserve much criticism; however the products that have been introduced since 2007 are nothing like the products of twenty years ago, and in many cases the fees have been reduced to as little as 0.5 percent. *This is on average about one-third of what the average mutual fund loads, fees, and expenses run.*

EIUL contracts employ the same advantages of EIA annuities; however, they are wrapped around life insurance and offer a death benefit along with tax-free growth. These contracts are usually found in the companies' executive offices for the few and privileged top brass. These contracts are structured in the form of deferred-compensation vehicles. They allow companies to pay large sums of cash into EIUL vehicles where executives can grow and compound large sums of money tax-free. But I have news for you—the common person can do this, too, if he or she knows what to ask for. The company executive knows he will access the cash later via policy loans on the cash value; and because the IRS does not deem loan proceeds earned, passive, or portfolio income, there is no tax on the growth and the compounded gains. The executive never has to make any loan payments, and with the death benefit of the contract, the loans are paid off when he dies. Also, in most states, the cash values are all creditor and lawsuit proof.

EIUL vehicles are commonly tied to stock market performance and lock in gains when the stock market does well; they then hold their ground when the market is falling. See the example below. It amazes me that although these EIUL vehicles have been out for several years now, only seldom do I speak to clients who know the benefits and value of these sophisticated investments. Consider the 10 year period charted below from 1999- 2009

Value of 100k invested in the S&P 500 vs. EIA

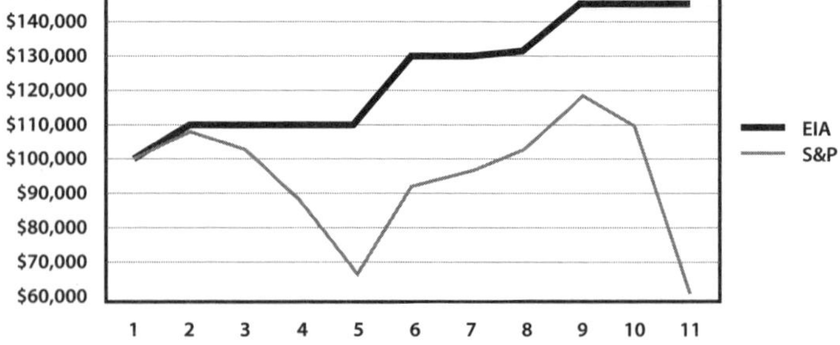

Example: Compare an EIUL contract and a common brokerage firm account over a three-year period. The market is up 10 percent in year one, down 15 percent in year 2, and up 5 percent in year 3.

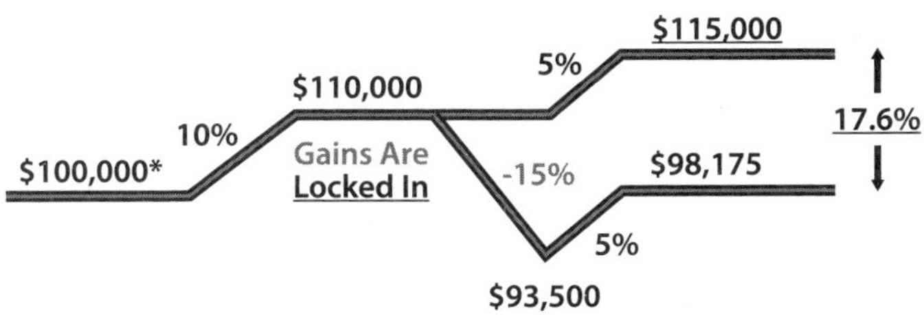

The EIUL locks in the gains in up years and does not participate in the down years like money at risk in an actively traded account.

Why do executives use this strategy to become rich when the common American does not? Fiscal literacy!

Note: I recommend that you work with a team of professionals to determine the most suitable and optimal mix of investments given your personal situation, including risk tolerance. Make certain to work with advisors who understand and appreciate the value of protecting your nest egg. You should not be "all in" on any one asset class be it real estate, stocks, bonds, annuities, or life insurance.

Money in the Market

For the money that you do have in the market make sure you work with an advisor that knows how to improve returns with financial strategies like Covered Calls, Absolute Returns, Counter Correlated Asset Classes, Private Money Management and Stock and Option Hedging. If you get a blank stare, or if the Advisor can only offer up the company menue of mutual funds, it's time to start looking for a new Advisor !

Fiscal Literacy Points

- The masses invest in home equity, mutual funds, and 401(k)s. The wealthy invest in fiscal literacy, building businesses, real estate, protected paper asset accounts, such as Wall Street structured investments, insurance and fixed annuity EIAs, and EIUL contracts that grow wealth and protect against market losses. Limit naked positions in stocks and mutual funds to dollar amounts that you can afford to lose if the markets turn downward.

- The wealthy invest in tax-favored and tax-advantaged vehicles.

- The average American only earns 4 to 6 percent on their investor returns and risks everything to do so.
- The wealthy and the educated do not risk their principal and still enjoy the stock market upside in concentrated positions.
- "Assets under management" are the primary focus of Wall Street.

Chapter Seven

Kids and Money: Seven Practical Lessons Every Kid Should Master

My personal goal for my children is that, by the time they leave our home, they will have a head start with money. My kids go to good schools, and I have been pleased to see some simple and basic life-management skills taught there, and even some applications with money; however, it would be naive to think that I could outsource these lessons to their teachers.

Parents must take charge in teaching money principals to our kids. This can even be fulfilling and fun for everyone in the home. Too often parents feel inadequate, go numb, or are just too busy to ever take action with the important financial lessons kids desperately need. It should come as no surprise when young adults stumble and fall into the common money dysfunctions that are the epidemic norm for Americans today.

Parents who are dysfunctional with financial concepts generally bring up kids who later become dysfunctional themselves. Parents, let me get frank here: *There is enough good information in this and many other books that you can use in your homes to ensure that your kids get a head start with fiscal literacy. There are no excuses anymore.*

Listed below are the primary areas that I recommend you begin with as you teach your kids money management principles. Kids should learn about:

- Giving;
- Maintaining a bank account;
- The manner in which the government collects taxes;
- Investing;
- Compounding values of money;
- Paying themselves first; and
- Cash flow management.

Giving

Learning to give is the key to abundance in your own life and in the lives of your kids. When your kids see you give to those in need, they see that generosity and compassion underpin your values, actions, and thoughts. Let your kids see your generosity with others. Tell them why you are giving at church or to someone in need. Let them help you in giving your time, money, and resources; and encourage them to give their own money, time, and abilities. The best way to teach your kids these values is by modeling them in your own life, not talking to them about one thing and then doing another.

I want my kids to have rich lives, which—despite our topic—has very little to do with money. I want them to experience abundance in their relationships, in their professional endeavors, and with what has been given to them. I want them to understand that they came into this world with nothing, that they will leave with nothing, and that the way to live an abundant life is not by scarcity or miserly thinking.

By being generous with your wealth, you will attract more wealth and abundance to you and your children, and you will live a more significant and satisfying life. There are so many good causes to support today. Find causes that impact your family and support them together. Unsure where to begin? Start with the local church of your faith or community organization.

Maintaining a Bank Account

Opening and maintaining a bank account is a healthy activity for any kid who is at least twelve years old. My bank sends my kids daily e-mails about the activities in their accounts (and copies me on the e-mails). My kids use debit cards, and I really like how they see what is going on in their accounts each day. To my chagrin, we really are becoming a cashless society; but I figure we had better get used to it and learn to work with money in an electronic age. By the time your kids are old enough to open bank accounts, understanding the simple plus/minus aspects of a basic bank account should come very easily to them. When the time comes, call your bank and let them know you are coming in to open custodial accounts for your children. Take your kids with you and have them fill out the application and make the initial deposit.

In my family, we do not allow our teenagers to have credit cards, so this will be a separate issue that they will learn to work with as they are leaving the nest. My kids must prove they can run a bank account before they will be considered for a credit card!

In talking with parents who have had trouble with older kids and credit cards, I have found that parents like to blame the credit card companies for their kids' problems when they arise. Just once, I would like to hear a parent say, "My kid ran up his credit card at college because he was a spoiled irresponsible brat with no discipline, and I was too busy with my own affairs to ever teach him how money works and what real life consequences feel like." Usually, a parent in this situation gets mad, yells at the kid, blames the credit card company, and then pays off the bill. The cycle repeats itself again and again until the kid returns to the nest (your home), ill-equipped to deal with managing money in the real world. *Now there is motivation for you to get this right, parents!*

The issue is sometimes not money at all; it is raising responsible kids. Responsible kids are usually good with money, and irresponsible kids usually blow it. To teach responsibility, you must incorporate stiff penalties for poor financial choices, just like in the real world. Do it now while the consequences are manageable. Do it later and the results might be as serious as foreclosure, bankruptcy, receivership, and financial and emotional dysfunction. Adult and senior parents are bailing out "kids" in their twenties, thirties, and forties all over this country, and that is a crying shame.

Taxes

Do you remember getting your first check and asking what the heck FICA was and what all those deductions were for? Get out one of your payroll checks and show your kid how much you make and what the government takes. Explain FICA and federal withholding. If you are fuzzy on the details, look them up before you try to explain. Get started by telling your kids what the government uses the money for. Show them your 401(k) deduction and explain what it is. Turn off the TV or PlayStation once a month to show them your family P&L (refer to chapter 2), and have them help you reconcile your monthly family cash flow. Get some buy-in from them, and don't be surprised if you develop some real connections with your kids. They will become more confident as they learn how things work with money in the household. It is a good feeling when you see your kids begin to care about what things cost. They will appreciate that you are treating them like grown-ups and including them in the family's important financial affairs, and this attitude will increase their willingness to cooperate with you when it comes to keeping an eye on expenses. Teaching your kids about money is hard work and will require a plan and probably some help, too. Parents, your kids are worth it!

Investing

I believe that kids today are too busy to get their heads around the more complex and sophisticated investment strategies that I recommend in this book, such as real estate (commercial or residential), structured and protected accounts, private placement, EIUL and EIA accounts, and leveraged portfolio accounts. Don't even try to go there with young teens or children. A bank account is a form of an investment—albeit a lousy one—and so are stock trading accounts. I have assisted my kids in opening custodial stock accounts with a local discount broker firm. My kids have bought shares in companies like Starbucks, Under Armour, AT&T, Frontier Oil, Fannie Mae, and others that they connect with in some way. We only started them with a small amount of money. The primary goal was for them to learn firsthand how an investment account works and to learn a little about stock fundamentals. We want to start simple with individual stocks so that our kids will later appriciate how more complex investment strategies can improve their results. (Refer to chapter 6 for more on this.) My son's Fannie Mae stock gained about 80 percent before the company was taken over by the government and the stock became worthless. He saw firsthand how he had no control over his money, no protection from downside, and no leverage or tax benefits. He did have a winner with Under Armour which he promptly remembered and bragged about. He seemed to forget about Fannie Mae. I see this with adults all the time. They remember the stock where they had the big score, and forget about all the losers that dragged down the blended result.

I believe kids develop confidence by learning and doing. They learn really fast, too. With one quick lesson my thirteen-year-old could navigate his online investment account with ease. He checks it after school and now wants to know and talk more about money and investing. My daughter is less interested, but she is in the game nevertheless; and I believe she has gained insights and confidence as well. By nature, she is more conservative and cautious than my son.

After kids have mastered cash flow management, saving, giving, and handling money responsibly, I recommend helping them with the investments this book teaches as they mature and reach adulthood. Partnering with one of your kids in a real estate investment or another investment structure seems like a great idea to me!

Compound Interest: Money on Steroids

Present your child with this simple scenario: Assume you are offered a job that is to last thirty days and the employer offers you two choices on how to be paid. Choice A is ten thousand dollars per day for each of the thirty days, and choice B is one cent for the first day, two cents for day 2, four cents for day three, and so on. Which method would pay more money? Give your kid a sheet of paper and tell him or her to figure it out. Their math will prove that Choice A would pay three hundred thousand dollars for the thirty days and choice B would pay about five million dollars. Such is the power and magic of compounding interest.

> *The most powerful force in our universe is the power of compound interest.*
>
> ~ Albert Einstein

Another vivid illustration of the power of saving and compounding to share with your kids is below.

Example: Lisa and Larry both save $1,000 per year ($83.33 per month or $19.23 per week). The money each of them saves earns 10 percent interest per year. Lisa starts at age twenty-two and stops at age thirty. Larry starts at age thirty and stops at age sixty-five.*

Age	Lisa Invests ($)	Growth	Larry Invests ($)	Growth
22	1,000	1,100	0	0
23	1,000	2,310	0	0
24	1,000	3,641	0	0
25	1,000	5,105	0	0
26	1,000	6,716	0	0
27	1,000	8,487	0	0
28	1,000	10,436	0	0
29	1,000	12,579	0	0
30	0	13,837	1,000	1,100
31	0	15,221	1,000	2,310
32	0	16,743	1,000	3,641
33	0	18,418	1,000	5,105
34	0	20,259	1,000	6,716
35	0	22,285	1,000	8,487
36	0	24,514	1,000	10,436
37	0	26,965	1,000	12,579
38	0	29,662	1,000	14,937
39	0	32,628	1,000	17,531
40	0	35,891	1,000	20,384
41	0	39,480	1,000	23,523
42	0	43,428	1,000	26,975
43	0	47,771	1,000	30,772
44	0	52,548	1,000	34,950
45	0	57,802	1,000	39,545
46	0	63,583	1,000	44,599
47	0	69,941	1,000	50,159
48	0	76,935	1,000	56,275
49	0	84,628	1,000	63,002
50	0	93,091	1,000	70,403
51	0	102,400	1,000	78,543
52	0	112,640	1,000	87,497
53	0	123,904	1,000	97,347
54	0	136,295	1,000	108,182
55	0	149,924	1,000	120,100
56	0	164,917	1,000	133,210
57	0	181,409	1,000	147,631
58	0	199,549	1,000	163,494
59	0	219,504	1,000	180,943

60	0	241,455	1,000	200,138
61	0	265,600	1,000	221,252
62	0	292,160	1,000	244,477
63	0	321,376	1,000	270,024
64	0	353,514	1,000	298,127
65	0	388,865	1,000	329,039
Value at retirement		$388,865	Value at retirement	$329,039
Less total contributions		$(8,000)	Less total contributions	$(35,000)
Net Earnings		**$380,865**	**Net Earnings**	**$294,039**

Lisa invested $8,000 total and saved $1,000 per year for 8 years. Larry invested $35,000 total by saving $1,000 per year for thirty-five years. But Lisa comes out ahead by $86,826!

Use simple and clear illustrations with your kids and watch the lights come on! Teach them to start investing early.

The lesson is essentially this: When you save or invest, your money earns interest or appreciates. The next year, you earn interest on your original money and on the interest you earned in the first year. In the third year, you earn interest on your original money and the interest you earned in the first two years. This continues until your money has multiplied and compounded with an unstoppable force. The three most important keys are1) to start young and use the free gift of time; 2) to start with what you have since even fifty or one hundred dollars will go a long way; and 3) to leave your money alone and let it grow. Use emergency funds for emergences. This stuff is hands off. Let it grow until you have enough to get into a real investment!

You Pay You!

Paying yourself works—but why? Simply because we all tend to spend what we have and what is available to us.

Kids' discretionary money can work the same way. Most kids (and parents) will continue spending until their money is gone. No matter how much comes in, we'll find some fun activity or new thing to buy with our discretionary money. Extra money can run through our fingers like water. In some families, expenses consume all the money that comes in during the month and some of the funds on the credit card as well.

Paying yourself first turns this problem into a winning strategy. If you take 10 percent of your income and put it in a savings account at the beginning of the month, you will be forced into spending 10 percent less each month. At the end of the month you'll still wonder where all the money disappeared to, but now you'll be able to rest easy, knowing that at least 10 percent of it is sitting in a savings vehicle compounding and growing in value.

For many, this can be a brilliant plan. Their spending seems to magically adjust to the available cash at hand, and the money grows and compounds with little effort. Teach your kids how to carve off a piece of their money for savings *before* they spend, and you may save each of them from a lifetime of financial dysfunction.

Cash Flow Skills for Kids

Learning to manage their own money can help children develop a sense of self-worth and confidence. Better to learn now than later, right? Every kid in America should develop a keenness for money traps and the tricks that advertisers play on them every day in this media-crazed culture.

This may sound crazy or heartless, but you should pray that your kids blow it and fall flat of their faces with money at an early age. These early lessons most often come at prices the family can afford, and the correction in the child's life arrives early enough to be well cemented in their minds.

Just like parents, kids should have income (allowance) and expenses. Each parent must determine what a suitable amount of money is for their child. This amount can vary based on the family's financial position and the age of the child. If the child is at least twelve years old, a bank account is usually a good idea provided the bank location is somewhat close to the home and the bank can offer a debit card and online banking.

I believe that parents should cover their children's needs—food, clothing, shelter, living expenses—and kids should be responsible for their wants—video games, trips to the movies with their friends, iPod downloads, and the like. By the way, I always pay for my kids when my family goes to the movies, out to eat, or to the ice cream shop, but if the kids are on their own, or with friends, these treats are on their nickel.

Another good idea is teaching your kids that Mom and Dad will only pay for reasonable clothing expenses and then having the kids pay any extra costs associated with a premium brand. For example, if we agree that the family budget for athletic shoes is fifty dollars, and my son wants a premium brand that costs eighty dollars, I will pay fifty, and he must pay the additional thirty. If he wants to save his money, he might agree to a pair that costs just fifty dollars. Either way, I want him to have skin in the game on the decision. In business dealings later in life, he will appreciate requiring his partners to have skin in the game.

Kids, just like parents, should track income and expenses with a monthly P&L (see chapter 2). Go to www.WeRetireWell.com and print off the family P&L or income and expense form. Kids as young as eight can handle this simple way to write down what they spend and what they bring in each month. This form is great for tracking money given, money spent, and excess cash to save. The kids (and parents) will see how much is going out the window for things the child will later reflect upon and appreciate—or perhaps look back on with regret. Here is where the lessons are learned early and where the rubber meets the road. Don't let this important opportunity pass you by, parents.

As kids become preteens and teenagers, they will have more opportunities to make money and to spend money. Allowing them to have skin in the game with financial decisions will teach them the value of money in a real and meaningful way. Some kids will be spenders, and others will be savers. Some will want to buy every new and shiny gadget that advertisers dangle in front of them, and others will be savers by nature. The only way for kids to have a reference for and an understanding of the value of money is for them to deal with money in the many of the same ways that you must deal with money. Too many parents attempt to shield and protect their kids from financial concerns. Just go to any high school in any decent part of town and look in the parking lot. Most of the BMWs and Mustang convertibles will belong to kids who have no idea what the value of money is or how to use it wisely. Mom and Dad pass out credit cards, cell phones, designer purses, and eight-hundred-dollar prom dresses like candy these days, unaware that passing out drugs could be just as harmful.

A recent study reported that of thirteen thousand college students interviewed, more than half had accumulated five thousand dollars or more in credit card debt while in school, and one-third owed over ten thousand dollars to credit card companies. Their parents must have been financially dysfunctional themselves, or they were too busy at the office or on the golf course to invest in developing fiscal literacy for their kids or themselves.

Many parents just want their kids to have it better than they did. They want the kids to have the things they've work so hard for themselves, but these parents fail to understand that they are robbing their children of the opportunity to build self-esteem by learning the fundamentals of cash flow management. Why should a kid care what anything costs if the First National Bank of Mom and Dad gladly picks up the tab every time? *Parents, don't let this be you!*

Fiscal Literacy Points for Kids and Parents

- Kids should learn to be responsible and accountable early.
- Generosity attracts abundance.
- Cash flow management is the key to wealth.
- Always pay yourself first!
- Compounding money has magic results.
- Kids must gain confidence early with money, finance, and investing.

Chapter Eight

For Seniors and Their Children

Seniors today have more threats to their estate and more complicated financial issues to deal with than ever before. Seniors are facing difficult choices with their money and their lifestyles. This can be extremely stressful and worrisome as they approach retirement and reflect upon how they will navigate the unique challenges that getting older in America brings today. These challenges include:

- Taxes, estate, income, tax on Social Security, capital gains tax;
- Income tax, eroding their estate (Estate taxes are 45 percent.);
- Probate, conservatorship;
- Long-term care costs, fear of nursing homes, and the nursing home spend-down

program;

- Rising medical and prescription costs
- Inflation, living longer, and the possibility of running out of money and becoming a burden to their children;
- Stock market losses and the low rates of CDs; and
- Legacy planning for children and charities.

Seniors need and deserve the very best in planning and structure to provide for safe and happy retirements. Most have worked hard all of their lives, raised families, and in my view, built and defended this country over the past fifty years and deserve our utmost respect and gratitude. Most have a nest egg or series of assets they have accumulated and many face grave challenges that threaten a secure and comfortable retirement.

Nothing saddens me more than to see American seniors taken advantage of by the Wall Street establishment. I have seen many senior portfolios that include hefty percentages of stocks (high risk) and hefty percentages of bonds and CDs (low returns). Some seniors feel that they have nowhere to turn and do not know whom to trust. It is unacceptable to me to see seniors lose large portions of their investments regardless of the size of their portfolios.

This chapter will provide the solutions that are common in the more informed and more affluent senior market. Affluent seniors have access to the very best tax attorneys, asset managers, and senior planning specialists. Affluent seniors effectively bypass many of the pitfalls that threaten the secure and comfortable retirement that every senior deserves. They use trusts, protected accounts, durable powers of attorney, LLCs, tax planning, MECs, EIAs, and stretch IRAs.

Informed and affluent seniors enjoy better returns than CDs offer, and they reject most stock market risk. Their estates have been structured to avoid probate and pay minimum estate and income tax so that they can pass on a legacy to their children rather than giving away their estate as a parting gift to Uncle Sam. Their income planning has been secured with protected accounts, and they choose MECs and linked benefits that cover long-term care without having to dig into their pockets for the expense. They have secured the necessary medical and POA directives so that in an emergency their decisions and wishes will be carried out and a court won't end up deciding important and critical decisions for them. Their planning has provided peace of mind, more choices, greater opportunities, better quality of life, more time with family, and in the end, more significance in life. This chapter will show you how they do it!

Taxes

Believe it or not, seniors are taxed out the wazoo. Just ask any senior. Of course there is the income tax that will never go away, and the current estate tax of 45 percent, as well as capital gains taxes. There is tax on just about everything seniors buy, but few know that seniors can also be taxed on municipal bonds that are supposedly tax-free. How so? Because the income counts toward the Social Security tax. Many people go into retirement and have no idea that their Social Security will be taxed. To understand this let's go back in history a bit.

In the 1930s President Franklin Delano Roosevelt launched Social Security. He stated that "as long as [he] live[d]" Americans would receive *tax-free* their Social Security benefit that they had paid into the system over their working years. Then what happened?

He died.

Back then, average life expectancy was in the fifties. Now people are living well into their eighties. As you might expect, the government changed the law in 1984 and assigned up to a 50 percent tax on Social Security. In 1993 the government changed the law again, and made Social Security benefits taxable up to 85 percent. Many seniors today are questioning what the government will do next with a system that is strained beyond its capacity. Most seniors today feel like their Social Security benefits will be further watered down in the years to come. This concern along with low CD returns, and stock market losses have gripped many seniors today who are concerned that they might last longer than their money will. Seniors are concerned about running out of money and becoming a burden to their children. After all, today if you make it to age sixty-five, you have a one in four chance of living to be one hundred.

Below is a chart on how seniors are currently being taxed on their Social Security benefits.

Single	> $25,000	= 50 percent tax
Married	> $32,000	= 50 percent tax
Single	> $34,000	= 85 percent tax
Married	> $44,000	= 85 percent tax

Today, with tax planning and deferred accounts, many seniors are able to minimize or avoid Social Security taxes altogether. Many seniors use equity-indexed annuity (EIA) contracts to defer income and change their bracket, rendering their Social Security benefits free from income tax.

Here's an example: Sam was taking in twenty thousand dollars per year from CDs. Sam did not need that money to live or meet expenses, so he just told the bank to roll the income back to the CD. In a review of his tax returns, Sam's advisor showed Sam how he could defer the CD income and lower his taxable income bracket. As a bonus, Sam's Social Security tax went to zero rather than 50 percent taxable. One simple adjustment in strategy lowered Sam's taxes significantly.

Age to Receive Full Social Security Benefits

Year of Birth	Full Retirement Age
1937 or earlier	65
1938	65 and 2 months
1939	65 and 4 months
1940	65 and 6 months
1941	65 and 8 months
1942	65 and 10 months

Year of Birth	Full Retirement Age
1943–1954	66
1955	66 and 2 months
1956	66 and 4 months
1957	66 and 6 months
1958	66 and 8 months
1959	66 and 10 months

Congress is currently looking at increasing the age that Social Security will become available.

Linked Benefits for Long-Term Care

Mary and Ed have a $100,000 CD. They don't anticipate needing the CD in their retirement, as they have sufficient assets in other accounts, as well as Social Security and a pension to meet income needs. In a review of their assets, Mary and Ed determine that they want to leave the CD to their daughter Lisa. In working with a senior financial advisor, Ed and Mary learn that they can move their money into a modified endowment contract (MEC), an insurance product, and immediately create $200,000 in death benefit that can pass on to their daughter Lisa tax-free. With $100,000 repositioned, they will be able to avoid probate and leave Lisa $200,000 tax-free upon their deaths.

Mary and Ed had looked at long-term care but decided to pass because the expense was so large. A recent AARP study they had read about reported that after age sixty-five, the chance of going into a nursing home was over 60 percent. Mary and Ed feared that all of their money could end up going to the nursing home and that they would not be able to leave their daughter any inheritance at all. They also feared that, if there was any money left, the government might take too much and leave Lisa with nothing. They were delighted to learn that an MEC contract would allow them to access up to 80 percent of the future death benefit ($160,000) if they were to ever need the money for long-term care.

A $100,000 CD transferred into a modified endowment contract life insurance policy would result in a $200,000 death benefit for their daughter Lisa; and $160,000 of the $200,000 (80 percent) would be available for Ed or Mary if needed in the future for long-term care.

I believe that, with the myriad of issues and concerns facing seniors today, sophisticated estate planning and structuring are paramount to ensure a smooth and comfortable retirement. I believe that seniors *deserve* that. Seniors face rising medical costs; medical expenses are rising faster than the cost of fuel, food, or just about any other fixed cost that a senior might face. Certainly, most people who make it to their eighth decade experience age-related health challenges. The average seventy-five-year-old has three chronic health conditions, and the list of chronic diseases that are linked to aging seems endless. Heart disease, stroke, cancer, diabetes, Alzheimer's, Parkinson's, and arthritis are just a few. The combination of rising medical costs and longer life expectancies is a legitimate risk to every senior's estate. Fortunately there are some great tools available today for seniors who are choosing to invest in fiscal literacy.

Market Risk

Barbara and Larry worked hard and raised four kids in Texas. Larry had never earned a large paycheck, but Barbara and Larry were wise with their money and always lived below their means. By the time Larry retired in the mid-1990s, he and Barbara had accumulated several hundred thousand dollars for their retirement, and the stock market was going crazy. Even though Larry knew the stock market involved risk, the high returns his golfing buddies were bragging about were too good to pass up. Larry moved a large portion of the couple's money into mutual funds, and even traded some speculative stocks now and then. For a couple of years, Larry was golden in all that he did with the family's money. Larry grew their portfolio by over two hundred thousand dollars. Then things took a sharp turn downward in 2000, and for the first time, Larry lost money. Reasoning that the time to buy was when the market had pulled back, Larry purchased more stock in an effort to make up for the money he had lost. In 2001, Larry lost even more money—quite a bit more. Larry was suddenly down from the point at which he had first begun several years back. In 2002, the bottom fell out, and Larry lost half of all the money that he and Barbara had accumulated for retirement. Now defeated in the stock game, Larry sold all of his stock and mutual fund positions and converted to cash.

There are millions of Larrys all across America who have experienced some version of this story. The stock market leaves a bloody trail for all but a few with the luck of the Irish who seem to magically get in and out at precisely the right time. Just like Vegas there are always a lucky few who do win … but we all know that Vegas was built on losers' money.

Some turn to CDs, but CDs seem to come with their own set of problems. Remember chapter 3? In most economic environments, people are aware that CDs struggle to keep pace with inflation; however, they forget that the forecasted inflation numbers (core inflation) strip out food and energy costs. I don't know about you, but my family is definitely paying more these days in food; and filling up at the pump has been a killer. If you add back these cost increases *real* inflation is much higher than the government's posted figures for core inflation.

Let's Look at an Example:

A $50,000 CD earning 5 percent interest earns $2,500 in one year and is taxed as earned at 30 percent. ($750.00 dollars are paid in taxes.)
$50,000 + $2,500 interest = $52,500
$52,500 – $750 (taxes) = $51,750 net, net
But we have inflation to deal with.Our $51,750 now only buys us 96 percent of what it did last year. $51,750 × 96% = $49,680

Great! We "invested" and effectively turned $50,000 into $49,680. Tell me again, how do we get ahead like this? Most seniors today are actually losing money in CDs due to inflation and taxes.

The more affluent and the more fiscally literate a senior is today, the more likely he or she is to reject stock market losses and poor CD returns. Many seniors have found out how to have their cakes and eat them, too. They secure lifetime income streams with EIAs and structured investments. Some have guaranteed income rates without risk as high as 6 to 7 percent with principal protection.

Take a look again at a simple chart from our chapter 6 on asset optimization. Tell me, which choice is more suitable for a senior? In the next example, consider that, while liquidity is important, our primary focus in investing is for income in retirement. A qualified advisor can help you determine what a suitable asset mix would encompass. Most families are too heavily weighted in asset classes that represent too much risk. Consider what can be accomplished in guaranteeing income in retirement with a fixed annuity. A fixed annuity with an income rider can give guaranteed returns to the income value of the account and allow the principal to participate in market returns. One might realize about 60 percent of the stock market gains to the accumulation value of the account and never ever lose any money when the stock market goes down. This is how an FIA account works. Note that the accumulation value may be less than the income value.

S&P 500 Actual Returns
LAST TEN YEARS
(2008 Estimate)
(S&P is a trademark of McGraw-Hill)

or

Guaranteed Fixed Account
7.2-PERCENT INCOME VALUE
FIA Structured Hybrid

Our investor must decide how to invest $100,000.

Wall Street		
Year	**Change**	**Amount**
1999	+19.51%	$119,510
2000	-10.14%	$107,391
2001	-13.04%	$93,387
2002	-23.37%	$71,562
2003	+26.39%	$90,449
2004	+9.00%	$98,589
2005	+3.01%	$101,645
2006	+12.8%	$114,655
2007	+3.81%	$119,023
2008	-35.00%	$77,364

Protected Account		
Year	**Change**	**Amount**
1999	+7.2%	$107,200
2000	+7.2%	$114,918
2001	+7.2%	$123,192
2002	+7.2%	$132,061
2003	+7.2%	$141,569
2004	+7.2%	$151761
2005	+7.2%	$162,687
2006	+7.2%	$174,400
2007	+7.2%	$186,956
2008	+7.2%	$200,423

**2008 Results are estimates at this time.*

END RESULT

Wall Street **$77,364**	**Protected Account** **$200,416**
Down 23% Over Ten Years	Average Rate Of Return
Return average: -2.3 percent per year	Return average: 7.2 percent (Income Value)
Effective average loss: 3.8 percent	Almost 3 times the performance No losses, no fees
(includes management cost of 1.5 percent)	
Client risks everything!	Principal Protected Accounts
Income at 6% per year = $4,700 year	**Income at 6% per year = $12,000 year**

So, to recap, protected accounts (EIA annuities) allow your money to grow tax-deferred. This means that all deposits plus interest earned grow tax-free, so the compounding effect on your money is even more powerful than that of a taxable investment. Simply put, your money grows faster! Recent revisions to Social Security tax rules provide for a reduction in taxes by realigning municipal bonds and other investments into annuities. By contributing to certain qualified plans (such as IRAs or SEPs) in the form of flexible annuities, pre-tax income is reduced, resulting in a tax savings. Protected accounts on average yield a return 3 percent higher than that of certificates of deposit (CDs). Protected accounts have no loss of principal and interest gain is indexed to the S&P 500 and/or NASDAQ. Most protected accounts allow a withdrawal of 10 percent of the present balance without penalties or fees. Unlike riskier investments, EIA annuities are principal protected and are considered to extremely safe. Your funds are always guaranteed in an annuity. Annuities bypass the very costly and time-consuming process of probate. There are no sales charges with EIA annuities, and all of your money is invested as opposed to being applied to sales charges and fees. Seniors today have no business whatsoever in the stock market gambit where they could lose most or all of their money. They simply do not have enough years ahead of them to make up for the losses.

Value of 100k invested in the S&P 500 vs. EIA

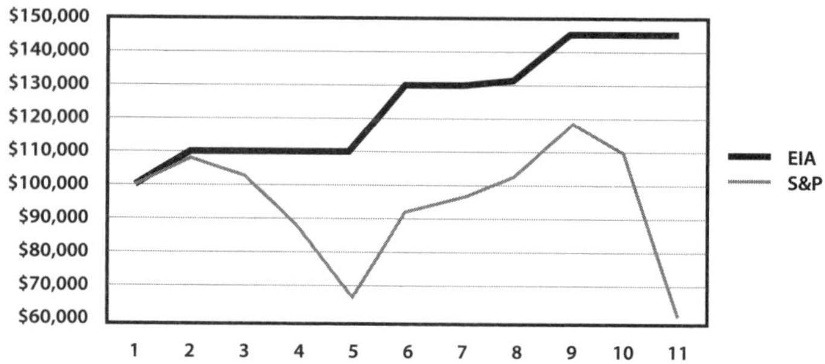

Wills, Trusts, and More

The estate tax is currently 45 percent. This one really gets me going! You work all your life to accumulate a few things. You pay tax on the money you make; you pay tax on the things you buy; and you pay tax on the returns that your money makes when you invest. I believe that after you have paid all of these taxes, your money is your money, right? Wrong! The government believes that your money is the government's money. They even tax you when you want to give your money away to your kids! If you do not have an estate plan in place today, do not worry—the government has one for you: probate and a 45-percent estate tax.

Smart lawyers protect and minimize their clients' estate tax with trusts (family and living), properly structured wills, LLCs, irrevocable powers of attorney, and certain financial instruments such as a linked benefit options. Seniors would be well advised to work with a well-qualified estate planner and an estate planning attorney to structure the proper will in their home state and/or a suitable trust so as to avoid probate.

Attorneys will often use a revocable living trust. A living trust is a legal document that you as the "trustier" create, after which ownership of assets is transferred to the trust. In this set-up, you also act as the "trustee" and maintain control of the assets; and you are the "beneficiary" of the trust, so you still benefit from the assets just as before. This document allows you to design the final distribution of your property after your death, just like a will, but your property bypasses the lengthy and expensive probate process. Unlike with a will, your financial affairs remain private upon your passing.

A pour-over will is a safety net that is created to ensure that all of your assets that are held outside your trust are "poured over" into your trust. This replaces your existing will and gives you a backup for any property that is not owned by your trust. A living will document expresses your desire not to have your life prolonged by artificial means if your death is imminent. A "directive to physicians" is helpful when you prefer to die with dignity and not to be kept alive by machines, while preserving your estate from rapid depletion due to extraordinary medical costs.

A financial power of attorney is a legal document in which a *principal* grants an *agent* the authority to deal with the principal's assets or properties. This power of attorney can be durable if the agent's authority continues in the event that the principal is disabled. A healthcare power of attorney document grants another person (your agent) the power to make healthcare decisions on your behalf, when you are unable to do so yourself because of a disability. This document can help to avoid the living probate process of guardianship hearings.

Wills, trusts, and related topics are discussed further in chapter 9.

Estate Executors

Who usually gets named the executor of an estate? The good kid, right? The one who always did his homework and ate his vegetables. Instead, you should name the troublemaker and get him back—it's your last chance!

Probate can be an expensive and time-consuming. Below are some of the responsibilities that your executor will have in probate.

Executor's Primary Duties

1. Probate of will
2. Advertise grant of letters
3. Inventory of safe deposit box
4. Claim for life insurance benefits; obtain Form 712 from insurance company

    a. Consider mode of payment

5. Claim for pension and profit-sharing benefits

    a. Consider mode of payment

    b. Obtain copies of plan, IRS approval, and beneficiary designation

6. Apply for lump-sum Social Security benefits and VA benefits
7. File Form 56: Notice of Fiduciary Relationship
8. Open estate checking and savings accounts
9. Write to banks for date of death value
10. Value securities
11. Appraisal of real property and personal

property

12. Obtain three years of U.S. individual income tax returns and three years of cancelled checks

13. Obtain five years of financials on business interests plus all relevant agreements

14. Obtain copies of all U.S. gift tax returns filed by decedent

15. Obtain evidence of all debts of decedent and costs of administering estate

16. Determine whether any of the decedent's medical expenses were unpaid at death

17. Determine whether the estate has received after-death income, taxable under Section 691 of the IRC

18. Prepayment of state inheritance tax (Check state law to determine if permissible and advantageous and if the applicable deadlines.)

19. Consider requesting prompt assessment of decedent's U.S. income taxes

20. File personal property tax returns (due February 15 of each year in administration)

21. File final state individual tax return (IRS

Forms 1040 & 706, due April 15 of the year after the year in which death occurs, and gift tax returns, due by the time estate tax return due)

22. Determine whether the estate is subject to ancillary administrations

23. Determine whether there are administration expenses and losses to be claimed as an income or estate tax deduction

24. Obtain alternate valuation date values for the federal estate tax return

25. Payment of U.S. estate tax with flower bonds (must be tendered to Federal Reserve with form within 9 months of death)

Legacy Planning with Your IRA

In estate planning today, many seniors are choosing legacy opportunities such as a multi-generational IRAs or stretch IRAs that pay out benefits over the lifetime of their children and grandchildren. A senior once told me that he viewed his IRA as an IOU to the IRS! The trouble with no planning being in place is that the senior's IRA account will go to the primary beneficiary after the surviving spouse passes unless special arraignments are made before the owner's death. When a beneficiary inherits an IRA, the entire value is treated as "ordinary income." The total amount will be added to the beneficiary's reportable income in the year in which this happens, potentially increasing the taxes on their *entire* income. The advantages of multi-generational planning include:

- No mandatory distribution for your children, eliminating the mandatory taxes on all income over a five-year period;
- Utilizing tax laws to make your IRA a multi-generational IRA, allowing you to increase the payout from your IRA to as much as five times its original value (assuming a 5 percent rate of return);
- Creating a lasting legacy, a lifetime of income for your family; and
- Generating peace of mind that your years of saving will not be depleted by the IRS.

Legacy Planning with Your IRA

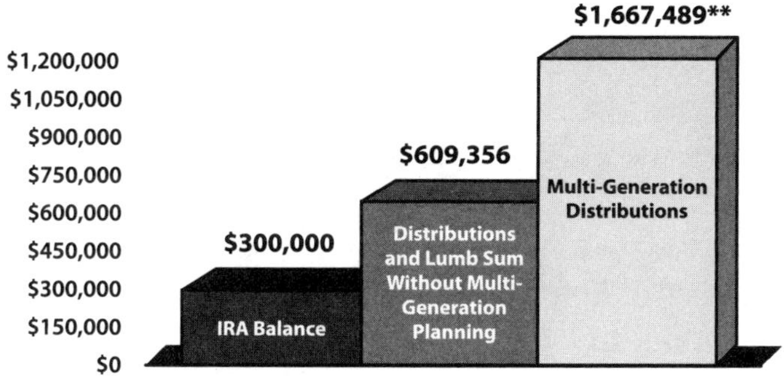

* This program is available for qualified money and non-qualified as a spendthrift program

** Assuming a 5% rate of return (3% minimum guarantee) using current mortality tables.

The stretch IRA is one of the most important components of any sound estate and legacy plan. Benefits, payouts, and distributions are commonly paid out at as much as five times the original IRA amount because the distributions are made over the lives of children and grandchildren. Seniors are well served to work with professionals who understand the unique needs and concerns of people at their stage of life. Seniors too often do not have sufficient assets to garner the time and attention of the Wall Street brokers whose main concern is assets under management.

When was the last time that your financial advisor called you up and said, "Hi! Let's get together and go over some strategies that will protect your estate, lower your taxes, increase your income, and provide innovative solutions to the high cost of long-term care."? Be honest—you don't get that call, do you?

Seniors, I recommend that, as soon as possible, you find someone who expresses an interest in helping you navigate the complicated financial and legal maze of senior issues—and has the credentials to back it up. Do it while you can, while you still have all of your faculties. Don't procrastinate. Time is precious. Seniors, the tools are available for each one of you to increase the quality and safety of your retirement plan, your peace of mind, your standard of living!

Note: I recommend that you work with a team of professionals to determine the most suitable and optimal mix of investments, given your personal situation, which includes risk tolerance. Make certain to work with advisors who understand and appreciate the value of protecting your nest egg. You should not be "all in" on any one asset class, be it real estate, stocks, bonds, annuities, or life insurance.

Fiscal Literacy Points for Seniors

- The government has an estate plan for you: probate and a 45-percent estate tax!
- Build your own estate plan to avoid probate.
- Reject stock market losses and CD mediocrity.
- Utilize MECs and Fixed EIAs for growth, safety, and income.
- Stretch your IRA benefits.
- Safeguard your estate against inflation.

Please t that the author and his affiliates do not advise on any personal income tax requirements or issues, and the author is not a licensed tax advisor. Any information from this publication or the associated Web site is for general information only and does not represent personal tax advice of any kind either expressed or implied. You are encouraged to seek professional tax advice for all personal tax questions and assistance. IRS tax guidelines change regularly.

Chapter Nine

Wills, Trusts, Estate Planning, Legacies, and Giving

Right now over 70 percent of Americans do not have a will. That's about 200 million people. Why? "Too busy," "Gonna get around to it," and "Can't afford it," are the top three excuses slackers give. Give me a break! I am not talking about single homeless people with nothing to lose. I am talking about Middle America: your neighbor, your friend, or you. The wealthy have wills, trusts, and estate planning in place because they understand the importance and stakes of protecting their estates, their personal wishes, and their children. The higher one's level of fiscal literacy and financial education, the more likely one is to have these important elements in place. Mind you, I'm talking about fiscal literacy and financial education—*not* intelligence. I have a very smart friend with an MBA and degrees in chemistry and engineering who told me that a will has been on his to-do list for years. He falls in the gonna-get-around-to-it category.

Without exception one of the biggest mistakes I see in personal finance is the lack of a will that has been properly drafted by an attorney in one's home state. *You don't just need a will, you need the right will.* Hear me loud and clear: Your California will is insufficient in Texas, and your Texas will not serve your wishes in the way that you want in Florida. The thirty-dollar will-writing software program that we can all buy at Wal-Mart will not get the job done because each state has its own probate, conservatorship, and intestate succession methods and procedures. This point has been driven home to me by at least three of the country's leading estate planning attorneys who have been enriched by probating estates with improper will and trust structures. My sister, who is a top attorney in Michigan, will not give family members freebies on their wills because she's busy and we live in Texas. Don't be cheap on these important financial documents. You should expect to pay a few hundred dollars to protect your estate, your family, and your peace of mind.

Parents, if you have children, you should write a will in order to appoint guardians for your minor children and trustees to manage their property. In some families there may not be a good choice as to who should get the kids if something happened to both parents; however, it is critical to press on and select the best possible choice. This one difficult choice shuts many families down altogether, and they never make a decision and form their will. *The stakes are too high to drop the ball here.* If you do not leave a will, the court may appoint a guardian—even someone who might have been one of your last choices. I cannot imagine a worse event than our kids being awarded at the court's discretion. We all owe it to our families to have this done the right way at once. Naming a guardian for your minor children is one of the most important considerations in your will. If only one parent dies, the surviving parent will remain responsible for the children; however, things can get challenging if mom and dad die at the same time or if a surviving parent remarries. Again, if you do not name guardians for your minor children, the court will decide who takes custody of your kids.

Your will spells out who will get your money and who will get your kids, but those choices do not have to be one and the same. Your will can also prevent minor children from inheriting real estate by themselves. Although kids have the legal capacity to own property, in most cases they do not have the maturity to manage real estate. If your kids inherit a share of your home, business, or other property, there is a possibility that your spouse will not be able to sell it, rent it, or even restructure the loan without a court order. Court orders can be expensive, time-consuming, and stressful for everyone involved. Children usually do not inherit community property in the absence of a will, but they do inherit a share of your separate property; because of this you must be protected.

What if you died right now without a will? If you die *intestate*—without a will—what happens to your property will depend on your marital status and whether or not you have children. For someone who is married with children, the laws of most states award one-third to one-half of the estate to the surviving spouse. The rest of the property goes to the children, regardless of their ages. Most people believe that all would go to the surviving spouse.

For someone who is married with no children, most state laws give only one-third to one-half of the estate to the surviving spouse. The remainder generally goes to the deceased person's parents, or if the parents are dead, to brothers and sisters. If you are single with children, state laws uniformly provide that the entire estate goes to the children. In the case of a single person with no children, most state laws favor the deceased person's parents. If both parents are deceased, many states divide the property among the brothers and sisters. This often occurs after much time, money, and resources have gone into one to two years of probate. (Go back and reread the sections regarding probate in chapter 8.)

You might be surprised to find out that your spouse might not inherit everything in the event of your death. If you and your spouse have no children, your parents or siblings might inherit part of your home and become co-owners with your spouse. Your spouse would not be able to sell the house or other property without their permission and vice versa. If you want to remember your parents or siblings in your will, it is best to leave them specific pieces of property that they will not have to share with your spouse.

If you die without a will, all of your heirs will become *co-owners* of every asset you own and will have to manage all the property together. This is made difficult by the fact that they may not live in the same state, and they may not be able to agree on what should be done with the property. The more heirs you have, the more money and effort they will have to spend trying to get organized. With a will, you could leave specific assets to specific heirs, or put one heir in charge as trustee for the others. Either way, your writing a will will save your heirs significant hassle and expense. It could also prevent major feuding. In the absence of a will, real estate is likely to be inherited by minors or numerous co-owners, and either result will be costly.

Power of Attorney

When you have a properly drafted will drawn up by a qualified attorney in your home state, you will execute several other important documents such as a power of attorney, a medical power of attorney, and/or a physician's directive. A power of attorney is a document that appoints another person to make decisions for you regarding your estate and affairs in the event you are away or unable to do so. You can appoint any competent adult person, such as your spouse, a relative, or a friend. This could be very important to your spouse in the event that you are detained or incapacitated. A power of attorney gives your named agent the power to manage your financial affairs in the same way that you would freely be able to do yourself. Typically, this would include the ability to:

- Buy and sell real estate;
- File and sign tax returns;
- Open safe deposit boxes;

- Apply for government benefits;
- Transfer assets into trusts you created;
- Hire professional advisors;
- Conduct banking transactions; and
- Make loans on your behalf,

With a health care power of attorney, you name someone to be your agent, health care representative, or advocate who can make decisions for you regarding medical treatment, healthcare, and life-sustaining decisions in the event you are unable to make these decisions on your own. They might decide issues in any of the following areas:

- Anesthesia and pain management
- Refusing treatment, medication, or artificial feeding;
- Hiring someone to care for you;
- Releasing physicians from liability; and
- Releasing your health care records

You may also want to leave specific instructions on the level of care you want to receive. For example, you may want to authorize the withholding of life-sustaining treatment (a feeding tube) if you are in a coma or a persistent vegetative state. You can refuse treatment in the event of an incurable condition which, although it is not terminal, causes you to experience a progressive deterioration of your physical and/or mental condition and loss of faculties.

The bottom line is this: if you do not have will, properly drafted by a qualified attorney in your home state—*get one!*

Estate Planning

In 2006, the credit exemption amount increased from 1.5 million dollars to 2 million dollars. Accordingly, a decedent's estate must pay tax to the extent that the taxable estate is in excess of two million dollars. In other words, each person has a tax credit which can be used to offset estate taxes on the first two million dollars of assets. This credit will shelter transfers of up to two million dollars worth of property at the time of death. Gifts prior to death are exempt only up to one million dollars. Any lifetime gifts in excess of one million dollars are subject to gift tax.

The following schedule shows the estate and gift tax rates and the unified credit exemption amounts for future years:

Calendar Year	Estate and GST Tax Exemption	Highest Estate and Gift Tax Rate
2002	$1 million	50%
2003	$1 million	49%
2004	$1.5 million	48%
2005	$1.5 million	47%
2006	$2 million	46%
2007	$2 million	45%
2008	$2 million	45%
2009	$3.5 million	45%
2010	N/A (taxes repealed)	Top individual FIT rate (gift tax only)

Note: The Congressional bill that was passed in 2001, which provides for the estate tax to be repealed in the year 2010, automatically expires on December 31, 2010. Therefore, as it stands now, for the year 2011 and all subsequent years there will be an estate tax. Under the present law, if you die in the year 2010, there will be no estate tax due. However, if you die either before or after the year 2010, estate taxes will be imposed on all taxable estates.

Annual gifts of up to twelve thousand dollars per donor can be made and not be counted towards any of the tax credit amount. In other words, a married couple can give twenty-four thousand dollars per year to an unlimited number of donees without tax impact. This twelve thousand dollar exclusion is referred to as the "annual exclusion."

Fundamental changes were made in estate tax laws in 1982. Perhaps most important was the "unlimited marital deduction." This change in the law allows property to pass between spouses without estate or gift tax. Consequently, under the present tax laws, a spouse can leave his or her entire estate to the surviving spouse outright without taxation. However, this increases the estate of the surviving spouse so as to most likely subject it to tax. *Exhibit C* illustrates the unlimited marital deduction, as well as the problem it creates upon the death of the surviving spouse. As previously discussed, a trust is a separate taxable entity. By putting money into a trust, it can be kept out of the taxable estate upon the death of the second spouse. *Exhibit D* illustrates the use of the "family trust" to avoid tax upon the death of the second spouse. The "marital deduction trust" is frequently used in conjunction with the family trust to minimize estate taxes and to ensure that the funds in the trust will ultimately pass to the decedent's children. The "marital deduction trust" is also referred to as a "qualified terminable interest property trust," or "QTIP trust" for short. *Exhibit E* illustrates the use of the marital deduction trust in conjunction with a family trust.

In contrast to the family trust, the surviving spouse must be the only beneficiary of the marital deduction trust during her lifetime. Also, in order to qualify for the marital deduction when the first spouse dies, the trust must include the following provisions:

1. The surviving spouse must receive all the income annually. Hence, all trust income will be paid to the surviving spouse and therefore income tax flexibility is lost. Also, the surviving spouse must have the power to require that trust assets be made income-productive.

2. Principal distributions are not required. However, in the typical situation, the surviving spouse is given access to the principal for her health, support and maintenance.

3. Upon the surviving spouse's death, the trust assets are taxed as if they are part of the surviving spouse's estate. The deceased

spouse's estate must elect this treatment in writing when he or she dies. The taxes are paid by the trust when the surviving spouse dies, based upon the value of the trust at the time of such spouse's death.

4. Usually, the will of the first spouse to die specifies the distribution of after-tax assets upon the other spouse's death.

In larger estates, full deferral of taxes until the second death may have significant tax disadvantages. *Exhibit F* illustrates full tax deferral in an estate of six million dollars. Most of the estate will be taxed on the death of W, the surviving spouse, and the family trust seems relatively insignificant. It may be better, since the estate tax is a graduated tax, to pay some tax at H's death, rather than adding all of his taxable assets to the top of W's bracket. A serious disadvantage of full deferral is the loss of flexibility in income tax planning. As previously discussed, all income from the marital deduction must be distributed annually from the marital deduction trust to the surviving spouse. In our example, wife will have to report on her 1040 all the income from the one million dollars in the Marital Trust. Another problem with tax deferral is the effective increase in value of the assets after H's death. Significant value changes may result in a much greater tax if there is an increase in asset value after H's death. Under present tax laws, W can refuse all or part of the marital deduction gift and elect to pay some tax at H's death. This choice does not need to be made until after the first spouse dies. The election to refuse a portion of an inheritance is called a "disclaimer."

Thus far, we have discussed testamentary planning for the surviving spouse. Planning for the disposition of assets when both spouses are deceased is another important concern which is discussed below.

Second Generation Planning

In the case of very large estates, when property is passed to the children on the death of the second spouse, that property becomes part of the children's estate for purposes of computing the estate tax. In the case of large estates, this results in the imposition of estate tax on each of the children's estates. This can be avoided in large part by use of a lifetime trust arrangement in the parents' will as opposed to an outright distribution to the children.

The Tax Reform Act of 1986 provides for a "generation-skipping tax" on transfers from grandparents to children, whether directly or through a second-generation trust. However, each grandparent has an exemption from the tax of two million dollars. Thus, a married couple can pass four million dollars to their grandchildren tax-free while still allowing their children lifetime benefits through a trust. As with most irrevocable trusts, the trust property cannot be reached by claims of creditors or jurisdiction of a divorce court. Also, professional management assistance can be provided for the child through designation of a corporate trustee. *Exhibit G* illustrates second-generation planning.

Revocable Living Trusts

The revocable living trust is a method of transferring assets to a trust during a person's lifetime and, thus, avoiding probate on that person's death. The person who transfers his or her assets to a trust is referred to as the *grantor*. The person for whose benefit the assets are held is referred to as the *beneficiary*. Typically, a revocable living trust provides that the grantor and the beneficiary are the same person. In other words, a grantor transfers assets to the trust to be managed for his or her own benefit.

When a person transfers all of their assets to a revocable living trust, they technically do not own any assets upon their death, and probate is not necessary. The assets which are "owned" by the trust will pass in accordance with the terms of the trust. However, because in some states probating a will is a relatively simple process, there is often no significant advantage of a revocable living trust over a will. Your estate attorney can give you the specifics for your home state on this important issue.

Candidates for a revocable living trust include:

1. People who own property in multiple states. If a person owns property in several states, the use of a Revocable Living Trust can avoid "ancillary probate" in many states.

2. People with complex business ownership. People who own their own businesses and have a relatively complex business life often find that passing ownership and control of assets through at trust provides for a smoother transition than a Will.

3. People who desire to keep the affairs of their estates private.

In the probate process, a list of all assets of the estate is filed with the court. Any person who wishes to see this list may simply go to the courthouse to view it. With a revocable living trust, a list of the grantor's assets are not made public. However, it should be noted that relatives, creditors, and other "interested parties" may demand and receive a copy of the trust instrument and a list of assets of the trust estate. In other words, a Revocable Living Trust certainly does not guarantee one's privacy, it only prevents the automatic publication of a list of the estate's assets.

Effectively, setting up a revocable living trust is much the same as "probating one's will while one is still alive." The deed to all real estate owned by the grantor is transferred to the trust, all brokerage and bank accounts are transferred to the trust, and all other assets which a person owns are transferred to the trust with the aid and guidance of an attorney. Naturally, the attorney bills the client for the services rendered in transferring the assets to the trust. This is very similar to the probate process, except that in the case of a revocable living trust it is done before death, thus eliminating the need to do it after death.

Note: Every revocable living trust comes with a will which designates the revocable living trust as beneficiary of any assets not owned by the trust at the time of grantor's death. If the grantor dies owning any assets, then his or her will must be probated to get these assets into the trust.

Thus, the goal of avoiding probate is not met.

Exhibit C

Trusts
The Unlimited Marital Deduction
Outright Transfer to Spouse

$4,000,000	
H **$2,000,000**	**W** **$2,000,000**

H leaves $2 million outright to W. No estate tax is due.

Problem: Upon W's death, she has a taxable estate of $4 million (possibly more with interest, earnings and appreciation of assets).

Exhibit D

The Unlimited Marital Deduction
Family Trusts

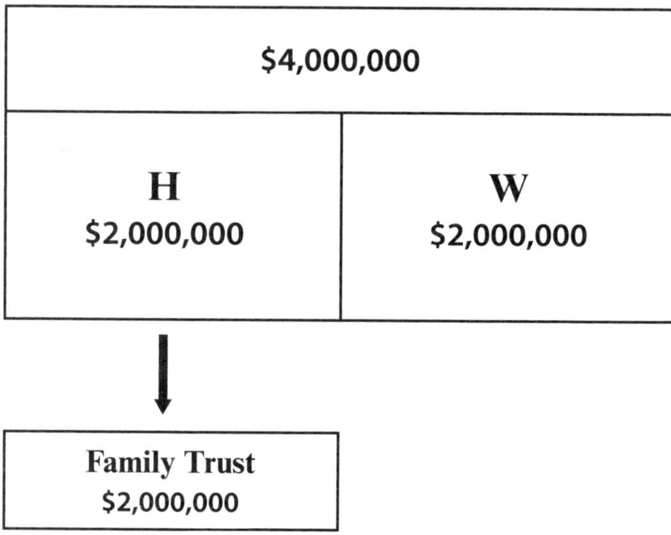

$2 million plus growth is never taxed.

Sample Trust Terms:

- Income plus principal to wife as needed.
- Remainder to children.
- Wife is co-trustee with her bank, and she can appoint a new bank if unhappy with present bank for any reason.

Exhibit E

The Unlimited Marital Deduction Trust

The "Q-Tip" Trust

$5,000,000	
H **$2.5 Million**	**W** **$2.5 Million**

↙ ↘

A	**B**
Family Trust **$2,000,000**	**Family Trust** **$2,000,000**

A. $2 million plus growth is never taxed.

B. $500,000 passing to marital trust is not taxed until W's death.

Note: The marital trust *must* provide for all income to be distributed to W annually, and W must be the *only* beneficiary.

Exhibit F

The Unlimited Marital Deduction Trust

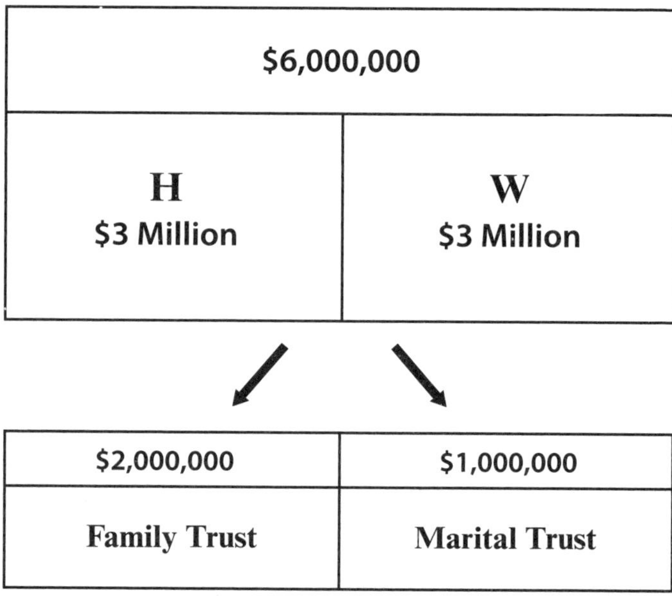

This arrangement:

1. Protects assets from divorce and creditors;
2. Shifts income to lower bracket descendants; and
3. Secures management assistance.

Fiscal Literacy Points

- Get a properly drafted will in your home state drawn up by a qualified estate planning attorney.
- Use estate planning principals to avoid estate tax—legally, morally, and ethically.
- Work with the best estate planning attorney in your community to develop your personal estate plan.

Legal disclaimer: *This book provides information about the law designed to help readers safely cope with their own legal needs. But legal information is not the same as legal advice—the application of law to an individual's specific circumstances. Although we go to great lengths to make sure our information is accurate and useful, we recommend you consult a lawyer if you want professional assurance that our information, and your interpretation of it, is accurate and appropriate to your particular situation. The author DOES NOT provide any legal advice and readers should consult with their own lawyer for legal advice.*

Chapter Ten

The Team: Tying It All Together

It is my sincere desire that by now you become better educated and more fiscally literate in several key areas of personal finance. I hope you have identified several key tax strategies that you and your tax planner will initiate immediately along with determining if real estate investing may be right for you. I hope you will choose to reject stock market losses in your portfolio, fire those advisors whose agenda is clearly articulated in the mutual funds that they recommend, and reject those advisors who may not be as fiscally literate as you have become through learning about the strategies contained in this book.

As I have stated throughout this book, all Americans deserve and need the all-star financial teams that will help them move up their financial freedom dates, when they will finally be doing what they want to be doing with their time. An all-star team has a quarterback, and that person is you. You must be in charge—no one else—but you need a team of advisors to protect you and help you advance the ball. You can't do it alone. I recommend having the following key players by your side:

- Tax attorney;
- Estate planner/attorney;
- Progressive CPA;
- Professional bookkeeper;
- Mortgage planner;
- Insurance professional;
- Real estate broker;
- Business attorney;
- Trusted financial advisor; and
- real estate attorney.

When you interview advisors I recommend that you ask them about their own teams. You might get lucky and have the opportunity to work with a financial advisor who understands the benefits of working as a team and has assembled this kind of a team already. Beware of advisors who are one-man bands and who try to do it all. These advisors will waste your time and your money and will likely have their own agenda for your money and *their* products. Enter your meetings with your advisors with an understanding of what is possible and available to you in the finance and investment world. Remember: there is no substitute for fiscal literacy and educating yourself with books such as this one and others that are not product-agenda oriented.

Interview your advisor first, before he or she interviews you, otherwise the advisor may just tell you what you want to hear. Let the prospective advisor know before your first meeting that when you meet you would like to go through a series of questions to help determine if you share the same philosophies. Be careful here, as most advisors will seek to interview you first, and then may simply give you the answers that they believe match your philosophies. Don't show your hand first!

Here are some questions to ask a potential financial advisor:

1. What are your qualifications?
2. What is the profile of your typical client?
3. Whom will I be dealing with at your firm?
4. What is the net worth of your average client?
5. Can you explain your philosophies regarding retirement and financial and estate planning?
6. How long have your been in business?
7. How many clients do you have?
8. How do you feel about mortgage debt?
9. What are some of the typical investments you recommend?
10. What is your personal net worth, and how do you build wealth for your family? (Don't be afraid to ask this one. Explain that you prefer to take financial advice from someone who has a net worth comparable to or higher than your own and with whom you share common philosophies.)

11. Why should I work with you and your firm?

12. Do you have any complaints filed against you?

13. What level of ongoing communication would I have with you and your firm?

14. Can you provide me with references?

15. Have you assembled a team?

After you effectively interview an advisor you will have an idea of whether you share common views and you will know whether he or she is a true professional. If you have an uneasy feeling, keep looking. Do not be surprised if this process is somewhat difficult for you. You may find that you are more educated in many ways than most of the mutual fund sellers you come into contact with.

I recommend working with independent advisors, as it is impossible for captive agents at the large wire houses to be objective with the products they recommend due to the captive nature of their employment. If XYZ Investment bankers are taking a new company public, guess which IPO all twenty thousand of their salespeople will suddenly feel is a good investment for their clients? Independent advisors have the freedom to recommend a larger and more diverse range of investments choices to their clients without being influenced by quotas from their employers.

Suitability

This book recommends mastering your personal cash flow, paying your fair share of taxes, maximizing your mortgage and real estate opportunities, developing good money habits, protecting your estate, and avoiding losses with your money. I have not provided specific portfolio recommendations here as there are too many factors to consider and each person has his or her own unique set of circumstances that must be examined to determine suitability. Instead, I recommend that you work with a team of qualified advisors, each of whom has his or her own specific niche and area of expertise. A good asset manager will not try to write your estate plan; the best CPAs will not be selling mutual funds in the side office; and your attorney should not be selling you life insurance. You must set financial goals and develop a plan with the assistance of your advisors to move up your financial freedom date. Set a date, make a plan, and expect to win!

Teamwork is the ability to work together toward a common vision. The ability to direct individual accomplishments toward organizational objectives. It is the fuel that allows common people to attain uncommon results.

~ Andrew Carnegie

Wheel of Fiscal Literacy

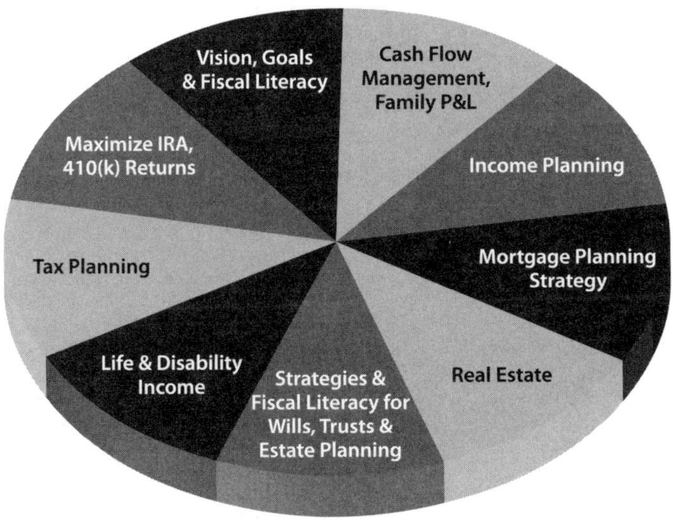

For addition information,
please visit my website.

www.WeRetireWell.com